Information Theft Prevention

As retail businesses migrate to the digital realm, internal information theft incidents continue to threaten online and off-line retail operations. The evolving propagation of internal information theft has surpassed the traditional techniques of crime prevention practices. Many business organizations search for internal information theft prevention guides that fit into their retail business operation, only to be inundated with generic and theoretical models. This book examines applicable methods for retail businesses to effectively prevent internal information theft.

Information Theft Prevention offers readers a comprehensive understanding of the current status of the retail sector information theft prevention models in relation to the internationally recognized benchmark of information security. It presents simple and effective management processes for ensuring better information system security, fostering a proactive approach to internal information theft prevention. Furthermore, it builds on well-defined retail business cases to identify applicable solutions for businesses today. Integrating the retail business operations and information system security practices, the book identifies ways to coordinate efforts across a business in order to achieve the best results. IT security managers and professionals, financial frauds consultants, cyber security professionals and crime prevention professionals will find this book a valuable resource for identifying and creating tools to prevent internal information theft.

Romanus Izuchukwu Okeke is a Research Fellow working as part of the Security and Information Systems Group (SIGS) at the School of Business, University of Central Lancashire in Preston, UK.

Mahmood Hussain Shah leads the Security and Information Systems Group (SIGS) at the School of Business, University of Central Lancashire in Preston, UK.

Routledge Studies in Innovation, Organization and Technology

Information Theft Prevention

Theory and Practice

**Romanus Izuchukwu Okeke and
Mahmood Hussain Shah**

Routledge
Taylor & Francis Group

NEW YORK AND LONDON

First published 2016
by Routledge
711 Third Avenue, New York, NY 10017

and by Routledge
2 Park Square, Milton Park, Abingdon, Oxon OX14 4RN

First issued in paperback 2018

Routledge is an imprint of the Taylor & Francis Group, an informa business

© 2016 Taylor & Francis

Library of Congress Cataloging-in-Publication Data
Names: Okeke, Romanus Izuchukwu, editor. | Shah, Mahmood, 1971– editor.
Title: Information theft prevention : theory and practice / by Romanus Izuchukwu
    Okeke and Mahmood Hussain Shah.
Description: New York : Routledge, 2016. | Series: Routledge studies in innovation,
    organization and technology ; 41 | Includes bibliographical references and index.
Identifiers: LCCN 2015039741 | ISBN 9781138841673 (hardback : alk. paper) |
    ISBN 9781315732015 (ebook)

ISBN 13: 978-1-138-61719-3 (pbk)

ISBN 13: 978-1-138-84167-3 (hbk)

Typeset in Sabon
by Apex CoVantage, LLC

Contents

Figures

Tables

Case Studies

Acronyms and Meanings

ABCP	Association of Business Crime Partnerships
ACFE	Association of Certified Fraud Examiners
ACPO	Association of Chief Police Officers
ACPR	Australasian Centre for Policing Research
APWG	Anti-Phishing Working Group
ATM	Automated Teller Machine
BRC	British Retail Consortium
BSBS	Basel Committee on Banking Supervision
CCA	Consortium for Cybersecurity Action
CCTV	Closed circuit television
CIFAS	Credit Industry Fraud Avoidance System
CRSA	Control Risk Self-Assessment
DBIR	Data Breach Investigation Report
DFRWS	Digital Forensics Research Workshop
DHCP	Dynamic Host Configuration Protocol
DPA	Data Protection Act
e-Business	Electronic Business
EISIC	Intelligence and Security Informatics Conference
EMET	Enhanced Mitigation Experience Toolkit
e-Tailing	electronic retailing
FCSA	Financial Crime and Service Authority
FSS	Forrester and Seeburger Security Services
FTC	Federal Trade Commission
GIA_DSE	Global Information Assurance and Data Security Essentials
GIAC- GSEC	Global Information Assurance and Security Essentials Certification
HTTP	Hypertext Transfer Protocol
IT	Information Technology
ID Theft	Identity Theft
ID Theft ADA	Identity Theft and Assumption Deterrence Act
IP	Internet Protocol
ISA	Information Systems Security Audit
ISACA	Information Systems Audit and Control Association

ISBS	Information Security Breaches Survey
ISO	International Organisation for Standardisation
ITRC	Identity Theft Resource Centre
MIS	Management Information System
MPS_OS	Metropolitan Police Operation Sterling
NFA	National Fraud Authority
OCSR	Organised Crime Strategy Report
PCeU	Police Central e-Crime Unit
PDA	Personal Digital Assistant
PIN	Personal Identification Number
PID/I	Personal Identifiable Information/Data
QPS_MFIG	Queensland Police Service Police Major Fraud Investigative Group
RBF	Role-Based Framework
SOCA	Serious Organised Crime Agency
SSH	Secure Shell
UK	United Kingdom
US	United States
UK ACAS	United Kingdom Advisory, Conciliation and Arbitration
UK AFI	United Kingdom Annual Fraud Indicator
UK CSS	United Kingdom Cyber Security Strategy
UK NAO	United Kingdom National Audit Office
UK ONS	United Kingdom Office for National Statistics (ONS),
UK_CDA	United Kingdom Crime and Disorder Act
UK_FAP	United Kingdom Fraud Advisory Panel
UK_HOCPU	United Kingdom Home Office Crime Prevention Unit
UK_NSDR	United Kingdom National Staff Dismissal Register
UNCPCJ	United Nations Congress on Crime Prevention and Criminal Justice
US DARPA	United States Defense Advanced Research Projects Agency
US NICCP	United States National Infrastructure Cyber Crime Program

Foreword

ABOUT INFORMATION THEFT PREVENTION: THEORY AND PRACTICE

A practical guide that addresses retail businesses' critical information concerns—theft of personal identifiable information/data (e.g., customers' details, trademarks, payment card details, personal identifiable data/information, trade secrets, bank account details, system configuration codes and details)—gives you a business advantage by directing your security strategies at their source: the people, their processes and technologies. A practical guide is about finding the right strategy that balances the protection of business information with allowing people do their job with efficient cost saving, high confidence, secured data integrity and increased productivity. Most businesses are aware of internal information theft and its consequences. Establishing a practical information theft prevention strategy is feasible, however, only if you know that the biggest obstacles you will grapple with in your retail business come from within your company.

This guide provides an in-depth understanding of key factors: the people, the process and the technology that play significant roles at the various stages of information theft prevention strategies, leading to successful implementation of security systems designs and tools. Combining interdisciplinary studies in computer security and criminology, the book consists of contributions focusing on theory, research and practice in the field of information systems security and human resource management. It generates an understanding of potential IS security loopholes and the counteractive theoretical and practical solutions for students, practitioners, financial fraud analysis researchers and university lecturers in the domain of the Information Systems Security. It also provides processes for the strategic delivery of IS functionality, prioritized based on business case studies, which ensures a proactive internal information theft prevention approach in business operations.

Preface

Whereas a majority of books on internal information theft prevention are wholly technical and bundled with abstract models, this book builds on well-defined models, theories, practices, and case studies that are fit for an in-depth understanding of critical issues of internal information theft prevention. Most importantly, it provides a comprehensive understanding of the current status of information theft prevention issues vis-à-vis the internationally recognised benchmark of information security.

The key benefit of this book is that it integrates information system research theories, models, practices and case studies for the purpose of information theft prevention. It identifies and contextualises theories for effective IS security; it recognises the best theories (e.g., Clarke's 25 Techniques, General Deterrence Theory, and Organisational Role Theory) and practices to be involved for better results; and it includes comprehensive analysis of information compliance practices between businesses, their policies and their operations.

This book equips information system security practitioners, academics, researchers, and students with knowledge of emerging concerns related to internal information theft in the domain of Business Information Systems Security. This guide directs readers who are concerned about internal information theft within and around their businesses. It does not only help you become aware of how your business can be vulnerable to internal information theft; it also suggests ways to help you prevent it. It is a practical, self-paced guide that provides basic security strategies as well as real-world prevention case studies, examples and helpful tips from business owners and security experts. Readers will find the guide easy to follow with an index for quick access and references.

About the Authors

Dr. Romanus Izuchukwu Okeke is a research fellow, working as part of the Security and Information Systems Groups (SIGS) at the School of Business, University of Central Lancashire, in Preston, UK. He has been a researcher in business information systems, systems and operations for five years. He has published articles in the *Journal of Basic and Applied Scientific Research* and *European Intelligence and Security Informatics Conference*. His research interests cover areas of identity theft prevention in e-businesses.

Dr. Mahmood Hussain Shah leads the Security and Information Systems Group (SIGS) at the School of Business, University of Central Lancashire, UK. He is the sole author of a new book on *Mobile Working* (Routledge, 2013) and co-author of *Business Information Systems* (Routledge, 2011), *E-banking Management* (IGI Global, USA) and has published papers in several high-quality journals, including the *European Journal of Information Systems* and the *International Journal of Information Management*. He leads a number of research projects in mobile security, identity theft prevention in online retailing and information security in e-banking.

1 Understanding Internal Information Theft

A Case of Retail Business

1.1. INTRODUCTION

This book is about preventing internal information theft in retail business. We therefore begin by answering an essential first question, namely, *What is information theft?* We answer this question by discussing the concept of information theft, and we contextualise the theft *within* retail business. The expected second question is, *Why should you bother with prevention of internal information theft?* We answer this question by looking at overall impacts—socio-economic costs of internal information theft in retail business. These discussions are directed towards building the background to a basic question—*How do you prevent internal information theft?*—which is answered by subsequent discussions in the rest of the chapters.

1.2. WHAT IS INFORMATION THEFT?

As it is expected from a fairly young area of research in business information security, there is not yet a universal consensus on the definition of information theft in retail business. We define information theft as stealing or an unauthorised access of personal identifiable details of someone else. For example, a retail company employee steals a customer's card details, market plans, product design, etc. for his or her own personal interest. However, several definitions are increasingly adopted, and it is probably fair that most researchers in information security (IS), when asked to provide their definition, will provide their understandings of information theft based on various concepts.

Researchers suggest that the problem with establishing a widely accepted definition of information theft is that different individuals from different business operations have different concepts. Others seem to be subjective to different ideas and experiences when they discuss information theft. In particular, a majority of researchers opined that a contextual meaning of information theft is a necessary, if not a sufficient, factor in the study of information prevention; and for information security experts, the contextual knowledge of information theft is a *must-have* for understanding its prevention. Hence, there is a need to underpin the identity and identification concepts and terms surrounding information theft.

Raab (2008, p. 3) expresses the concept of identity as follows:

> Identity and identification are not just specialist terms used only by researchers in our various technical discourses. . . . there is enormous and diverse literature that surrounds the term identity testifies to the growing importance of identity in the politics and social life of our time . . ., a fixed identity may be necessary if we are to function in daily life, and history attests to the severe difficulties that befall persons whose 'papers' have been destroyed or confiscated, and who therefore need to construct an identity . . .

The concept of identity as it is in the context of most social theory influenced the context of its discussion and analysis. Josselson et al. (2006) examined identity and states that: *"identities are not fixed and frozen" as individuals evolve in time"*. As defined by Burke (2008, p. 2), an identity "is a set of meanings applied to the self in a social role or as a member of a social group that define who one is". Koops et al. (2009) define 'identification of an individual' as it attributes to 'self' as a vital element of identity explanation. They distinguished between 'Idem Identity' and 'Ipse Identity', defining them as the 'sameness of persons or things' and 'personal identity in the meaning of an individual sense of self', respectively.

This concept of 'idem identity' is adopted in the rest of this study. Information thefts are committed against what makes an 'individual or an entity unique ', and this 'individual uniqueness' is what Goffman (1990) termed 'Identity pegs'.

1.3. INTERNAL INFORMATION THEFT: THE CONTEXTUAL ISSUES

Just as the definition of the term 'identity' is not straightforward, neither is the definition of information theft. The tactic adopted in this book is to answer relevant questions to simplify the understanding of the complexity of defining information theft. The basic questions that constitute important elements in defining information are: Who are the individuals or groups that perpetrate information theft? How is information theft perpetrated? When and where is information theft perpetrated?

To answer the above questions about the place and circumstances surrounding information theft, the discussion needs to be extended to retail business as an organisational entity with respect to management (people) and operations (process). The distinctiveness of information theft in retail business is also imperative to consider in discussing the prevention of this theft. This is because an extensive number of different information theft-related crimes often include the use or abuse of identity, which includes credit card number theft, cheque cards, debit cards and phone cards, ATM spoofing, pin capturing, database theft, electronic cash theft, as well as identity theft-related frauds such as counterfeiting, forgery, postal fraud, financial fraud and plastic card fraud.

As information thefts have different meanings in private corporations and in public sectors, some have argued that credit card fraud and account hijacking should not be conceptualised as information theft, as will be discussed in the various contextual definitions below. Specifically, most financial institutions classify fraudulent use of stolen credit card numbers not as an information theft but as a payment card fraud.

To answer the above questions, the UK Home Office Identity Fraud Steering Committee (2006) posits that information theft occurs when personal identity details are stolen by a thief to support unlawful activity. In contrast, security researchers in the United States define information theft as a takeover of someone else's personal identifiable information. In the same vein, in Canada, for instance, information theft must involve 'a deprivation of an actual thing to the owner', thus 'copying personal information from a computer or official document for criminal use.'

Many states, Commonwealth agencies and territories consistently use the terms 'identity fraud' and 'identity crime' interchangeably to explain the meaning of information theft. Adopting a general definition of 'identity theft and identity fraud', as put by the Federal Identity Theft and Assumption Deterrence Act USA, UK Home Office, and some researchers, might not be an acceptable or viable option. This is the reason for the general belief that the definition of information theft should be considered with respect to business context terms, location, region, and cultural background. However, some researchers argue that the most relevant issue is to explore the elements of these crimes and to relate them to the circumstances surrounding its occurrences with a particular business as an organisational entity. According to the United Nations Intergovernmental Expert Group (UNIEG) cited in the Organisation for Economic Co-operation and Development (OECD, 2008), in the term 'identity fraud', 'the element of deception' lies not only in the deception of technical systems and human beings to obtain the fraud but in the deception of victims in the subsequent use of the stolen information. However, there is still no standardised definition in the field of offences related to the theft of identity. As noted above, American literature always adopts the term identity theft to express information theft, whereas in the UK (HM Cabinet Office, 2002) and in other countries such as Canada and Australia, information theft can be described as the offence of identity fraud.

This difference in defining identity-related offences is still a big challenge in resolving the problem of information theft definition, as noted by Koops et al. (2009, p. 4):

> . . . It is also not clear what exactly constitutes 'information theft' and how these can be combated . . . This lack of precision becomes

especially apparent when comparing the various official media reports on these topics. Definitions are hardly ever provided, even though the statistics play a role in politically motivated discussions and policy decisions. Commonly accepted definitions are also lacking in literature. This means that we are at the stage where comparisons of apples and oranges abound making it virtually impossible to determine the real incidence of identity-related crimes . . .

Currently, the commonly cited definitions (although some could not be cited without critics) of information theft are as follows:

An individual is considered to commit an act of information theft when he or she "knowingly transfers or uses, without lawful authority, a means of identification of another person with the intent to commit, or to aid or abet, any unlawful activity that constitutes a violation of Federal law, or that constitutes a felony under any applicable state or local law.
(Federal Identity Theft and Assumption Deterrence Act USA, 1998, *title 18 United States Code—Section 1028)*

The UK Home Office defines identity theft as an act which

occurs when sufficient information about an identity is obtained to facilitate Identity Fraud irrespective of whether, in the case of an individual, the victim is alive or dead.
(Home Office Identity Fraud Steering Committee, 2006)

In a more extensive approach, the UK Fraud Advisory Panel (2011, p. 1) states that the term

'Identity fraud' is commonly used to describe the impersonation of another person for financial gain. Fraudsters steal your personal identity and/or financial information and use it to purchase goods and services or access facilities in your name . . ., it is the use of a false identity or another person's identity to obtain goods, money or services by deception. This often involves the use of stolen, counterfeit or forged documents such as passports, driving licences and credit cards.

In the Australasian Centre for Policing Research, James (2006, p. iii) defined identity theft as:

the theft or assumption of a pre-existing identity (or significant part thereof) with or without consent. It may involve an individual's identity (whether a person is dead or alive), or the identity of a business.

The OECD (2008) expresses the similarity in the definitions in stating that: 'information theft' is a subset of identity fraud and that both 'identity fraud' and 'identity theft' are a subset of identity crimes. Moreover, the contextual range of identity theft-related crimes are much broader and they are certainly significant as the definition is unrestricted to any particular context. This definition buttresses the point made Gerring (2001, p. 54) that

> a concept that applies broadly is more useful than a concept with only a narrow range of application'. A good concept stretches comfortably over many contexts; a poor concept, by contrast, is parochial—limited to a small linguistic turf.

In as much as the use of contextual perspectives surrounding information can be helpful to researchers in understanding the nature of information theft in retail businesses, the term 'identity theft-related crimes' is generally used in most literature (Meulen, 2011).

However, there are other terms used by researchers to describe information theft, such as 'identity deception'—which arguably is not widely recognised because the term 'deception' neglects the role of the victim whose personal identifiable information is stolen. Nevertheless, the definition of information theft in this book is the 'unlawful manipulation' of technical systems as well as human beings by dishonest or disgruntled employees to steal another person's identity to commit criminal offences. This book uses this definition as the basic reference for the subsequent subchapters.

The next sub-chapters explore some social theories which provide answers to questions about the nature of information theft in retail business as it is underpinned by the characteristics of perpetrators. Some vital theories that provide some interesting answers on 'why' motivations of information theft perpetrator are discussed, based on 'how', 'when' and 'where' these crimes are committed.

1.4. UNDERSTANDING INTERNAL INFORMATION THEFT IN A WORKPLACE

Over the decades researchers (e.g., Cressey, 1973; Ditton, 1977; Mars, 1982, 2006; Gill, 2011) have used theories to provide a comprehensive conceptual understanding of workplace theft: how thefts are perpetrated in a workplace, how organisations adapt to theft-related crimes and why the perpetrators act in certain ways. The theories discussed in this section provide this book with different 'lenses' through which to look at information theft.

For instance, Mars (2006) focuses attention on different aspects of the issues of occupational deviance: cheating, fiddles, pilferage, scams and sabotage in the 21st century and providing a framework within which to conduct their analysis. The analysis provides an understanding of the nature of information from the context of occupational crimes and relates it to retail companies.

This subchapter contributes to the understanding of the nature of information theft by providing answers to the question of *'why information theft'* in the retail businesses.

1.4.1. Internal Information Theft: Workplace Dishonesty

The evolution of the digital economy and changes in technology have direct impacts on the nature of workplace crimes. Computer-related crimes and internal information theft in this context are not the exception. Mars (2006) notes that, although the extension of information technology has undoubtedly reduced employee control in some jobs, it has radically increased their control in others. In his anthropological study of occupational crime, Mars (1974) applies Douglas's (1970) concepts of 'grid' and 'group' to classify occupational structure in relation to workplace deviance. He divides employees into four categories based on the structure of their occupations. The first category is 'the Hawks', the workers who manipulate organisational rules to their own advantage. The typical examples of such workers are 'the entrepreneurs, the innovative professionals and the small business owners'. The second are 'the Donkeys'. The Donkeys are highly constrained by rules. They respond to the systems that constrain them by breaking them, 'to fiddle or to sabotage the systems'.

The third category is 'the wolves'. Mars (1974, p. 2) expressed this category as *'the dock work gangs'*, or 'the work-and-pilfer'. They work in well-organised and highly regulated packs. Fourth are 'the vultures'.

Examples are writers and travelling salesmen who work primarily in a supportive and corporative base. Although 'vultures' are highly competitive and individualistic, they fiddle in ways because of the nature of their job. These above categories which emerge from Mars's (1974) study show 'cheats', 'fiddles' or 'sabotages' as being multifunctional. Mars (1974) suggests that workers under different categories engage in dishonesty or criminal acts so as to make an 'unequal reward systems a bit more even'.

Mars cited instances in which workers justified 'the fiddles' as being indicators of occupational success and status, as satisfying punitive measures against employers, as being antidotes for boredom, as being ways of avoiding the delays and perceived injustices of clumsy bureaucratic systems, and as ways of increasing control at the workplace. Mars's (1974) overall suggestion is that 'the dishonesty' at the workplace should be seen as being more than an index of employee dissatisfaction, that it should be seen as pointing to ways in which the criminal activities could be changed so as to bring employees into the centre of workplace control. Specifically, Mars (2001a) suggests that increases in control over the 'the Grid Donkey jobs'—as in the call centres of the today's online retail companies, for example, encourage dishonesty and deviance, particularly resentment fiddles.

Information technology, paradoxically, increases the power of such dishonest employees, who, if disruptive, can be resentful and prone to sabotage.

In his agreement to the above contentions by Mars (2001a), Hollinger (1997) points out that behaviours of the dishonest employees in this computer age represent merely a 're-tooling' of deviant and criminal activity. In other words, sabotage as a form of computer-related crime is not necessarily a new form of sabotage but a 're-tooling of the status quo'.

Mars (2006) suggests that a response to curb the behaviours of dishonest employees categorised above does not always prove to be effective. He noted that such behaviours need collective preventive action from workplace management in form of both *'coercive technology' and 'technical up-gridding'* (Mars, p. 289). The above analysis of Mars (1974, 2001a) shows the importance of employing broad interpretations in explaining workplace deviance behaviours such as internal information theft, and not totally ignoring the covert occupational institutions and systems.

Mars (1974, p. 204) argues that

> any management who introduce or propose a change to the workplace without considering covert reward systems are operating blindfold; examine and discuss 'the way fiddles produce their own set of social relationship in the workplace and gauge the effect that any planned change would have on them.

This suggestion, in particular, is important. It underpins the rationale for exploring the theoretical analysis of the motivating factors that induce dishonest employees into internal information theft.

1.4.2. Internal Information Theft: Perpetrators' Motive

Researchers (Newman and Clarke, 2003; Gill, 2011) noted that there are three major factors that induce the dishonest employees to steal the personal identifiable information. These include: a) Perpetrators concealment; b) Financial gain and rewards; c) Business environment; d) Economic Climate—Recession.

Concealment of the Perpetrators: Some perpetrators of information theft in retail companies have the mindset that such an environment avails them the opportunity to remain anonymous. Newman and Clarke (2003) noted that environmental factors offer substantial opportunity for crime, as summarised with the acronym **SAREM:** Stealth, Challenge, Anonymity, Reconnaissance, Escape and Multiplicity, shown in Table 1.1 below.

Financial Gain and Rewards: It is a general idea that personal identifiable information is a psychological construct used to identify particular individuals 'uniquely' (Cast, 2003). Personal information is a construct which has invaluable attributes of every individual. This definition points to the fact that victims of information theft have lost something more than just money; if the personal identifiable information (PII) of an individual could be conceived as a composition primarily of information that is unique, priceless and invaluable, then one perhaps begin to understand the motivation of

Table 1.1 Concealment as a Motivation for Internal Information Theft

SAREM	Concealment Attributes
Stealth	The perpetrators are almost invisible on the Internet, a condition for committing information theft (Denning and William, 2000).
Anonymity	With the information system being characterised with a decentralised database system which operates in an anonymised platform, this allows the employees to perpetrate crimes (Wortley, 1997).
Reconnaissance	This attribute is noted as perhaps the most important element that motivates criminals in most business organisations, as the information system makes it possible to scan thousands of database servers and even millions of personal computers that are connected, looking for the target victims.
Escape	This sums up other attributes owing to the crime-inducing aspects of the information system environment of anonymity, deception and stealth, thus making information theft in retail business difficult to be detected. Perpetrators perceive that it is easy to escape punishment (Ahuja, 1997).
Multiplicity	Unlike other traditional theft, which is relatively limited in nature, internal information theft can be multiplied exponentially because the perpetrator has access to a vast number of new opportunities.

information thieves. Clarke (1999) has conceptualised that personal identifiable information is a 'hot product' and that hot products attract theft. He demonstrated how personal identifiable information—a 'hot product', can be more prone to theft than others using the acronym CRAVED: Concealable, Removable Available, Valuable, Enjoyable and Disposable, as described in Table 1.2.

Retail Business Environment: Motivations in a workplace may be perceived as predispositions to particular behaviours and outcomes, reflecting the things employees want and the strategies chosen to achieve them (Thompson and Mchugh, 2009). Researchers (e.g., Lacoste and Tremblay, 2003; Newman, 2004) have identified business environments, such retail business (online retailing), as the major source that provides opportunity for individuals who steal personal identifiable information.

They classified the sources into two:

1. Collection centres,
2. Application centres.

Table 1.2 Financial Gains as a Motivation for Internal Information Theft

CRAVED	Financial Gain and Reward Attributes
Concealable	From the information systems (computer networks, intranet and Internet), one can steal personal identifiable information secretly without possessing it completely, and can do so from any accessible and convenient place.
Removable	With the intangible nature of PII, it is thus removable, movable and intrinsically vulnerable to interception and can be disguised to any desirable and intended forms by the criminals.
Available	The revolution of the Internet has made all information potentially available to everyone. Personal information and records are there for the taking. In fact, one does not even have to steal them. One can buy identification information as cheaply, breed other identification documents from them and then convert them into cash.
Valuable	Personal Identifiable information details (e.g., credit cards, bank passwords) in this current information society (e.g., retail and banking industries) is conceptualised as money. These are valuable items; thus they are targeted by criminals.
Enjoyable	Information thieves in a retail businesses are lured by the prospect of pleasurable living and rewards whenever stolen identities of the innocent clients or customers are converted into cash.
Disposable	Sutton, Cherney and White (2013) notes that the availability of a fencing operation enhances the chances of particular items being stolen. Unlike traditional stolen goods, with the attribute of continued possession increasing the risks of being caught, stolen information and the disposal of the PII is not so apparently pressing. The criminal continues to savour the gains of the stolen PII in hiding until the crime is detected.

The Collection Centre/Point in a business environment is where the criminals steal personal identifiable information; the Application Centre is the point of use. Examples of the collection centres include: a business office via company databases and paper or electronic documents, business transactions via workplace environment and personal computers, financial statements via credit/debit statement and Internet, and data mining via abetted hacking. Moreover, other researchers (Davis, 2003; Newman, 2004) summarised characteristics of information thieves in relation to a business environment and based on their criminal activities, as described in Table 1.3.

Table 1.3   Features of Internal Information Perpetrators

Category	Characteristics
Incidental	These are the amateur information thieves that take advantage of varied incidences—data leakages within the information systems, without any specific task-based intention (Perl, 2003).
Opportunistic	Amateur criminals with intention, without taking any risk. These criminals are not professionals, but they look for opportunities; if they get one, they would take it. In some cases they are referred as circumstantial or secondary thieves. These criminals often advance to professionals because of interest and financial gain from the initial act (Davis, 2003).
Professional	These are criminals with learned techniques with an in-depth knowledge of various methods to steal information (Morris II, 2004).
Gang	These are criminals in the form of an organised group, comprised of several experts from suitable fields (e.g., Computing, Psychology). This form of thieves is offensive with a high level of commitment (Newman, 2004).
Seller	These are thieves that sell personal identifiable information such as credit/debit cards, e-mail address, driver's licence, home address, etc.

Economic Climate—Recession: Gill (2011) argues that there is some evidence that characteristics of an adverse economic climate can lead to either an increase or a decrease in crime. Gill suggests that because there is a possibility of the unavailability of credit due the recession, there is a likelihood that such an economic climate will create opportunities for fraud. Leslie and Hood (2009) agree with Gill (2011) and argue that if dishonest employees have less disposable income during recessions due to redundancy during recessions, they would be motivated to indulge in information theft. In contrast, Yeager (2007) argues that there should be caution in supporting the hypothesis that recession leads to an increase in crimes. Gill (2011) also cautions that care should be taken in generalising his suggestion because different crimes are influenced by different issues.

Gill (2011) and Yeager (2007) suggest that it is necessary to look into other theories that discuss the criminal motive behind the increase in crimes. Various researchers (e.g., Cressey, 1973; Kantor, 1983; Black, 1987; Brooks and Kamp, 1991; Kardell, 2007; Clarke, 2009) have used theories to analyse other motivating factors and situations that could induce employees to steal personal identifiable information. It is important to look into some of the theories that motivate crimes because they provide an analytical explanation of an employee's behaviour based on the key elements: environments, situations and time. These elements (environments, situations and time) answer the key questions of where, when, why, and how as they relate to the nature of internal information theft. Some relevant theories include:

- Cressey's Fraud Triangle;
- Person Theory;
- Workplace Theory.

Cressey's Fraud Triangle Model: In his theory of 'the triggers' that lead to theft-related crimes, Cressey (1973) pointed out that each criminal has motives and opportunities that induce them to commit crimes. He models a 'Fraud Triangle' of which each side represents components of what causes the perpetrators to commit crimes. The three components are Rationalisation, Perceived Opportunities and Social Pressure facing the individuals. Cressey (1973) explained that rationalisation and social pressures are the key attributes that motivate the employees' attitudes towards crimes. Kardell (2007) also suggested that, whereas perceived opportunities might be managed by the organisations, rationalisation and social pressures are generally beyond the control of the organisations.

Person Theory: This theory uses the concepts of Opportunity, the Marginality Proposition, and the Epidemic of Moral Laxity to explain why some employees may indulge in internal information theft. This theory could be extended to the prevention of internal information theft through personnel exclusion.

The summary of the interpretation of these approaches is presented in Table 1.4 below.

Workplace Theory: This theory contributes by explaining the reasons that some businesses, online retail companies in this case, suffer higher levels of internal identity theft-related crimes. Hence, the analysis provided by the workplace theory, which is situation specific, could lead to the evaluation of different systematic strategies for controlling and preventing internal information theft.

Workplace theory explains the motivation of disgruntled employees who engage in internal information theft based on the concept of the Workplace Theory shown in Table 1.5 below.

1.5. PERPETRATION OF INTERNAL INFORMATION THEFT

Subchapter 1.3 has provided knowledge of concepts and theories of the nature of internal information theft in the workplace while identifying the importance of this knowledge in understanding the motives of internal information thieves. While it contributes, in part, to answering the question of why there is internal information theft in retail businesses, this

Table 1.4   Analysis of Internal Information Theft Motivating Factors with Persons Theory

Person Theory's Components	Explanation of the Pearson Theory in Relation to the Nature of Internal Information Theft
Opportunity	Cressey (1973) and Kantor (1983) claim that opportunity correlates positively with nature of internal information theft and other related crimes. In agreement, Kardell (2007) argues that minimised opportunity like constant surveillance over employees' activities could be an internal information theft deterrence. This theory pointed out that employees, as humans, have greedy instincts. And this could be translated to theft if there is an opportunity at the employees' disposal.
Marginality Proposition	This approach holds that the employee's degree of marginality could cause internal information theft within organisations (Clarke, 2009). Social isolation, little opportunity for advancement, short tenure, low rank in the organisational hierarchy, low wages, expendability, little chance to develop relationships, etc. are characteristics of marginal employees. Employees that fall in this category are more likely to indulge in internal information theft.
Epidemic of Moral Laxity	This approach postulates that moral decadence in society today leads to moral laxity in organisations (Clarke, 1999). Newman and Clarke (2003) support this concept and suggest that employees of decades ago possessed more trustworthy qualities than the employees of today.

subchapter looks more in-depth on the perpetration. It provides an understanding of who, how and when internal information theft is perpetrated, and who detects the theft in relation to its prevention. With increasing cases of internal information theft, business owners and researchers continue to ask: why is this risk growing? To answer this question, it is important to reflect on the motivations of internal information theft discussed in Subchapter 1.3.

Rationalisation, opportunity and social issues have been identified as the key motivating factors for perpetrating internal information theft. A greedy (social issue) employee working in an unsecure IT infrastructure (opportunity) believes (rationalises) that s/he may not be caught for indulging in the

Table 1.5 Analysis of Motivations of Internal Information Theft with Workplace Theory

Workplace Theory	Workplace Theory Explains Internal Information Theft
Perceived Fairness	This model points to a relationship between employees and perceptions of organisational fairness. Tucker (1989) notes that theft can be better characterised as a mode of social counter-control rather than a crime. In this context, information theft is seen as a response to the perceived deviant attitude of the employer. This theory argues that the exploitative behaviour of an employer is the cause of the stealing. Hence, employees' admissions of internal information theft might be associated with job dissatisfaction.
Climate and Structure	This approach is suggested by Brooks and Kamp (1991). It argues that organisational climate encourages a dishonest attitude (Johns, 1987). Employees' perceptions about the work climate, their co-workers, attitudes of their supervisors and management can send messages to them about whether the crimes might be condoned or not. Shearman and Burrell (1988) note that the structure of IT security affects the propensity of employees to steal the organisation data. The more complex the security of the information storage, the fewer cases of internal information theft.
Deterrence Doctrine	This concept holds that internal information will be more likely to be perpetrated in an organisation where there is low awareness of anti-crime policies. Kantor (1983) supports this approach that employees' behaviours are influenced by the threat of organisational sanctions. According to Greenberg and Barling (1996), the most effective variable of this approach in deterring internal information theft is the perceived certainty of punishment among other variables: perceived severity and visibility of punishment.

theft. The perpetrators would be motivated to act because of the nature of retail business operations which are carried out using the Internet—activity behind the computers. Other major motives include gambling lifestyles or pressing bankruptcy and debts. Having the opportunity to steal prepares the fraudulent employee to look for the situations that would pay off. For instance, some of the perpetrators, irrespective of gender, either obtain temporary employment for the sole purpose of internal information thefts or place organised criminals in the business organisations to gain knowledge of the firms' information systems in order to steal critical information. Hinds (2007) suggested that the structure of a firm's Information Systems and Data Protection Policy is among the key enabling elements that may encourage internal information theft. These elements are interrelated such that one situation or an opportunity for internal information theft may lead to another.

STRUCTURE OF INFORMATION SYSTEMS

Perpetrators of internal information theft often target and exploit weaknesses in retail business operation because of the structure of the information systems and the business policy. The modern information systems architecture of tye retail sector is often designed to store the customers' data in one place which could be accessible to employees in a variety of departments. It is generally built with a structure of distributed information systems in which networked computers communicate and interact with each other to achieve the common goal of their business transactions.

This design may result to the consolidation of diverse customers' information that might be of easy access to thieves (Duffin et al., 2006). It makes it easier and quicker for perpetrators to have comprehensive information about the customers' data at a glance. This structure also creates opportunities for organised criminals to target employees in the information system department of the retail companies.

DATA PROTECTION POLICIES

More than a decade ago, Judith Collins argued in the case of the US department of Justice that information theft-related crimes are escalating because of the lack of a definitive policy. Due to the definition problem in the context of internal information theft, some law enforcement agencies were not able to record internal information theft as a separate crime from other computer-related crimes. And because of the nature of computer-related crimes as cross-jurisdictional issues which may span or cover several geographical areas and business networks, the mitigation may have led to confusion about who is responsible for investigating and prosecuting such crimes.

In some cases, this leads to the victims of information theft reporting the cases to the wrong enforcement agencies. For instance, in the case of information theft involving bank details, victims are likely to report the case to the financial crimes investigation agency rather than to the police. The issue of undefined data protection policies and jurisdictional or management roles makes the loss related to internal information theft more impactful. For instance, most outsourcing firms run into difficulty in offering a personal identifiable information monitoring service for their customers because some employees within the retail companies thwart credit-monitoring processes based on the stipulations that the outsourcing firms (third-party firms) are not part of their statutory data protection policy. Such circumstances contribute to the identity monitoring service arriving days after these crimes activity have transpired.

1.5.1. Methods of Perpetrating Internal Information Theft

Researchers (e.g., Mitnick and Simon, 2006; Green-King, 2011) suggest that infiltration, collusion, coercion and social engineering are the common methods used by internal information thieves in retail companies. These methods can be carried out independently or combined with other mechanisms. For instance, with collaboration and social engineering, combined, internal information thieves can generate phishing web pages for nearly any online retail company at the click of a mouse or the tap of a key. APWG[1] (2014) suggests that some internal information thieves often succeed in manipulating the IS by using various techniques.

Common techniques include the use of unapproved hardware/devices, abuse of private knowledge, violation of e-mail/IM/web/Internet policy of the victims, handling of data on unapproved devices/media, storage/transfer of unapproved content and use of unapproved services/software. In addition, APWG indicates that a majority of the perpetrators use botnets to commit PID[2] account fraud and privacy counterfeiting, through networks of IS and machines with malicious programmes in the form of phishing attacks. Table 1.6 summarises common mechanisms for perpetrating internal information theft.

1.5.2. Other Methods of Internal Information Theft

Other methods used for stealing information are phishing, repairmen and elaborate yarns to hoodwink the human resources staff into providing the company's PII assets. The key technical modes used by the outsiders/external agents who were abetted by malicious insiders include malware, hacking, social engineering and physical actions. Although some online retail companies may implement elaborate authentication process, firewalls, networking security monitoring technology and virus scan software, their IS may still be porous to incidents of internal information theft due to collaborative and colluded practices of employees and external agents. In addition, with the aid of dishonest employees/insiders in the target retail company, the external agents and dubious information security experts and their accomplices could equip themselves with evolving technical tools to manipulate the systems.

Due to the *techie knowledge* of the employees (software engineers, IS/T administrator), they often exploit the IS weaknesses related to configuration,

Table 1.6 Common Mechanisms of Perpetrating Internal Information Theft

Methods	Explanation
Infiltration	This is a mechanism whereby organised criminals plant the agents in the retail companies. The planted criminals (outsourcing agents, vendors, and partners) could gain employment to commit internal information theft. The factor behind this method could be linked to the commercial pressure or to high employees turnover in online retail (Green-King, 2011). The pressure can open the door for an influx of deliberate criminals in retail outlets and call centres. Green-King (2011) suggests that less stringent vetting and recruitment control measures encourage infiltration. tc "Infiltration" \f C \l 1This situation is often difficult to detect. The perpetrators often resign before the detection. Some criminals lease or sell the compromised data.
Collusion	Organised criminals and the dishonest collude with fellow employees (in some cases with dismissed employees or business partners) who have access to personal and business information systems— payroll, account details, business transactions and records. It is a common approach used by some criminals of the same cultural background (Hinds, 2007). The meeting point is often at lunchtime, in nightclubs or pubs and at social events. tc "Collusion" \f C \l 1
Coercion	Organised criminals intimidate and threaten employees to partake in internal information theft-related crimes. In some cases, call centre employees of the same company are being threatened by the top managers. Some employees who become involved in this fraudulent activity often claim that they did so under duress. Successful coercion often leads to collusion with the collaborators.Hinds (2007) suggests that 45 per cent of the internal information theft cases in the UK are coerced, of which 15 per cent admitted to having been paid to compromise their customers details. Some of the innocent employees (e.g., cashiers and wait-staff) were often coerced to skim payment cards. There were reported cases of recruiting the IS/T administrator for the purpose of stealing data, opening IS/T holes and disabling security systems. Verizon DBIR (2013) indicated that pretexting was one of the common elements of social engineering modes used in information theft perpetration.

Methods	Explanation
Social Engineering	Act of pulling a con job to get access to an information system that is normally accessible by the privileged users—employees. Several researchers (Savage, 2003; Duffin et al., 2006) have noted that the perpetrators that use this method of internal information theft are often linked with an internal employee as an agent. This mode often involves social tactics—deception and manipulation—in exploitation of the roles of the human elements and end-users. These modes of information theft are often linked to both the technical and non-technical modes, alongside collusion of the perpetrators with external agents for successful exfiltration of victims' personal information. Checkpoint (2013) suggests that employees are paid in some cases to get access to critical business data/information, because the external agents perceive that stealing of personal identifiable information would be impossible without the aid of the internal employees.Check Point (2013) indicates that 42 per cent of UK companies have been hit by social engineering attacks and that new employees (52 per cent), and the outsourcing agencies and contractors (44 per cent) are the most vulnerable agents.
Patchable Software Vulnerability(PSV)	Verizon Data Breaches Investigation Report (DBIR) (2013) notes that PSV is one of the key methods of stealing business information and customers personal identifiable information (PII). Verizon DBIR (2013) discusses the summary of the Verizon DBIR from 2008 to 2013, which shows that web applications, remote access and desktop services are the commonest pathways or vectors through which PII could be stolen. This report emphasises the role of human errors when privileged users manage these vectors in online retail companies. This evidence shows that remote access and desktop services combined with exploitation of default/stolen credentials are very rampant in retail companies.It can be concluded that opportunistic internal information theft incidents (intrusions) are common in retail companies that often share the same IS/T support with software vendors. With knowledge of a vendor's authentication methods and schema (e.g., TCP port 3389 for RDP; or TCP port 5631 and UDP port 5632), internal information thieves (system administrators) can exploit (without traces) across the full range of the vendors/partners/outsourcing companies (Peretti, 2009).

functionality or application. The CIFAS (2011) and Verizon Risk Team Survey Report (2012) indicated that in the use of phishing (via pretexting and solicitation) as an information theft vector of choice, external cybercriminals relied on the personal touch, with more than 78 per cent of internal information theft cases involving in-person contact. They noted that even in the high-tech business world, all facets of cybercrimes would not get done without an in-person 'meet and greet'.

For some of these methods (e.g., social engineering and patchable software vulnerability) of carrying out internal information theft to be successful, Verizon's Data Breach Investigations Report (DBIR) (2012) suggests that the perpetrators have to depend on the insight provided by the insider, who may have comprehensive knowledge of the target retail companies.

In some internal information theft cases, these methods could lead to advance persistent threats (APT) techniques such as Distributed Denial of Service (DDoS), botnets and zombies, Social Network Attacks, Clickjacking / Exploit kits/Crime packs, Infected Near-field communication (NFC), Scareware—fake security software warnings. CSO Magazine (2011) agrees that in cases of information theft, those that were linked to APT were perpetrated through sending internal data information to the external site/entity, tampering with the command/control channel, disabling/ interfering with security control, stealing of login details, Sequel Query Language (SQL) injection and key-logging procedures and abuse of system access/privilege.

1.6. TARGETED ASSETS BY INTERNAL INFORMATION CRIMINALS

It is imperative to discuss internal information theft in relation to assets/data types. There was almost no report that indicated categorically the features of personal identifiable information/data (PII/D) stolen in retail businesses.

There were always issues of concern in relation to privacy of PII/D owners, mostly in relation to records containing names, e-mail address, source codes, etc. However, CIFAS (2013) indicates that the majority of internal information theft incidents involve stealing of the payment card information (containing names, e-mail address, source codes.) and authentication PID/I credentials. Dean et al. (2011) noted that some companies' product patent and formulas are often stolen by internal thieves and sold at the cheapest rate on online auction websites. Some are sold at about 70 per cent off the patented versions on the online black market. Table 1.7 shows the variety of compromised IS/T assets classified by those that occurred in all businesses (irrespective of the size) and in big business, and by PID/I name, incident and record.

Figure 1.1 derived from Table 1.7 shows a chart of the targeted personal identifiable information and assets which have the highest records

Table 1.7 Distribution of Targeted Assets by Perpetrators (Verizon Report, 2012)

Variety of Compromised PID/I	Label	All Business		Large Business	
		Incidents (%)	Records (%)	Incidents (%)	Records (%)
Payment card number	CardData	48	3	33	1
Authentication PID	PIDCredit	42	1	35	1
PID (Name & Address)	Personal	4	95	27	98
Trademark, TradeSecret	OrgData	4	1	37	1
Bank Account Number	BankData	2	1	10	1
System Info. (Config &Svcs)	SysInfo	2	1	15	1
Unknown	Unknown	44	1	2	1

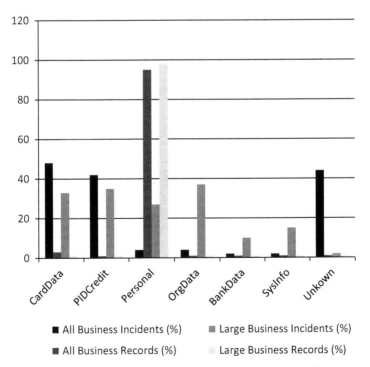

Figure 1.1 Internal Information Theft Cases across Large and Small Businesses

of compromise in both all and large business cases—95 per cent and 98 per cent, although these cases are associated with 4 and 27 respectively. In some cases, top business executives used their company's name to secure a fraudulent transaction. Sometimes these incidents bring brand dents to the company, not only financial lost. The Lloyds Bank ex-head is a typical instance. In June 2012, the former head of Lloyds' online security (Jessica Harper) was jailed for five years for internal information theft related to account-take-over and account-withdrawals. Jessica Harper was convicted for submitting some 93 bogus invoices.

1.7. INTERNAL INFORMATION THIEVES: WHO ARE THEY AND WHERE ARE THEY?

Metropolitan Police Operation Sterling MPS (2009) reported that employees who had been employed less than one year are more likely to collaborate with senior colleagues to steal personal identifiable information (PII). CIFAS (2011) suggested that some employees use their management positions and responsibilities because of their authority and access to unlimited information systems operations. Cases of internal information theft can be categorised based on the operation units of some retail companies.

From Table 1.8 below, retail stores, customer contact centres and field units are among the most targeted online retail business areas for information theft perpetration. This report corresponds with the Fighting Retail Crime Report (2012) which suggests that among 40 per cent of the companies interviewed, more than 25 per cent of their total internal information theft perpetrators were supervisors, security officers and senior administrators, of which 56 per cent held technical positions. Seventy-five per cent of

Table 1.8   Internal Information Theft Incidents versus Job Roles

Job Roles of Information Thieves	Percentage of Internal Information Theft Incidents (%)
Regular Employee/End-User	61
Finance/Accounting	22
Executive/Upper Management	11
Helpdesk	4
System/Network Administrator	2
Unknown	1
Others	1

the perpetrators were current employees and 65 per cent of these perpetrators occupied other positions with other companies.

Table 1.8, which was adapted from Verizon RISK Team Survey Report (2012), shows the distribution of internal information theft by per cent of incidents in relation to their employment position. It shows that regular employees and end-users are the categories of employees that are more likely to steal because of their job roles and operations.

Other examples of regular employees include corporate end-users—call-centre employees, who take advantage of their IS access/user privileges and use them to seek cashable forms of personal identifiable data/information (PID/I), such as bank account numbers and payment card data. This report suggests that information thieves need not be super-techie-users or the most trusted of information systems users to manipulate information systems.

While accounting/finance employees are noted to indulge in information theft due to their position or their accessibility to personal accounts and financial forms and records, IS administrators/developers have been noted as a significant per cent of the perpetrators. 'Others' in Table 1.8 means incidents of internal information theft indulged in by business partners and outsourcing firms.

Verizon RISK Team Survey Report (2012) also shows that in retail industry alone, 22 per cent of internal information thefts are perpetrated by partners/remote, vendors, and outsourcing companies who are responsible for managing the point of sale (POS). The Association of Certified Fraud Examiners (ACFE, 2014) agrees with this report and suggests that most internal information theft-related fraud schemes involve the accounting department or upper management. The ACFE (2014) indicates that more than 30 per cent of fraud cases are committed by the accounting department and over 20 per cent by the upper management or executive-level employees. The next commonly cited are employees from the digital marketing and sales departments. Forrsight Survey Report (2013) on the distribution of employees indulgent in information theft (in relation to department) agrees with the Verizon RISK Team Survey Report (2012).The Forrsight Survey Report (2013) indicated that the number of current employees abetting former employees in indulging in internal information theft is on the increase. Such perpetrators often sell the retail company's IS/T credentials (access codes, authentication processes, de-provisioning of user accounts procedures) to the online 'black market'.

The Forrsight Survey Report (2013) categorised 'likely internal information thieves perpetrators' in business organisations into four groups: Rogue, which comprises 9 per cent, HERO—the Highly Empowered, Resourceful and Operative Employees, comprising 16 per cent, Disenfranchised, which comprises 34 per cent and the Locked-down, with 41 per cent. This report suggests that Rogue and Locked-down perpetrators comprise 50 per cent of the total employees who pose the greatest internal information theft risks. The CIFAS Report (2013) suggests the following attributes of internal information thieves: male employees aged 25–30, fully employed, low paid, working in junior non-management, possibly in financial difficulties and possibly having worked in the victimised business organisation for less than a year.

CIFAS (2013) adds that 78 to 98 percent of intellectual properties theft out of overall internal information theft cases were perpetrated by male employees. This report corresponds with FraudTrack's (2012) report that intellectual properties theft cases are dominated by male employees, with women linked to 18 per cent of reported cases.

1.8. INTERNAL INFORMATION THEFT: THE RESULTING FRAUD PRACTICES

In most internal information theft cases, the perpetrators use the stolen assets for financial gain. In other cases, they use the stolen assets to create bank accounts or apply for fraudulent loans, or they sell the data on the black market. Fraudulent account withdrawals and account disclosure have become common fraud practices that result from internal information theft. CIFAS Report (2012) indicated that there is an almost 50 per cent rise in the number of cases of internal information theft compared to the previous years, which account for as many as 80 per cent of all computer and Internet related crimes.

Fraudulent Account Withdrawals: Fraudulent Account Withdrawals involve unauthorised access to or manipulation of customer account information details for personal benefit. Other practices linked with Fraudulent Account Withdrawals are fraudulent account transfers to the employee account and fraudulent account transfers to a third party.

Disclosure of Commercial or Personal data: This involves the use of a commercial or business identity's data without the consent of the data owner. The use of these data for unauthorised purposes always places the victimised companies and individuals at an operational risk and in financial difficulties, respectively. This is the case of the employee colluding with organised criminals to compromise customer data and information. The criminals could use the data to plunder the victim's account by making multiple applications in their names.

The UK CIFAS claims that intelligence from law enforcement agencies has unveiled the infiltration of organised criminal groups in businesses as responsible agents for the disclosure of commercial and personal data.

In a summary of the common forms of fraud practices resulting from internal information theft, the UK Fraud Advisory Panel classified common types of internal information theft-related crimes into two categories: corporate information theft and personal identifiable information theft. Table 1.9 summarises the two categories.

Table 1.9 Categories of Internal Information Theft

Category of Information Theft	Common Types and Schemes
Corporate Information Theft The impersonation of another company for financial or commercial gain. Fraudsters steal a company's identity and/or financial information and use it to purchase goods and services, obtain information or access facilities in your company's name.	**Company hijacking:** A fraudster submits false documents to a retail company to change the registered address of their employer company and/or appoint 'rogue' directors. Goods and services are then purchased on credit, through a reactivated dormant supplier account, but they are never paid for. **Company Impersonation:** A fraudster impersonates a retail company (sometimes by purporting to be a director or key employee) to trick customers and suppliers into providing personal or sensitive information, which is then used to defraud the retail company. In some cases, the retail companies may be impersonated using phishing e-mails, bogus websites and/or false invoices.
'Personal identifiable information theft' is commonly used to describe the impersonation of another person for financial gain. Personal identity criminals steal your personal identity and/or financial information and use it to purchase goods and services or access facilities in someone's name. This scheme uses a false identity or another person's identity to obtain goods, money or services by deception. This often involves the use of stolen, counterfeit or forged documents, such as passports, driving licences and credit cards.	**Application Fraud/Account Takeover:** A fraudster applies for financial services (e.g., new credit cards or bank accounts) using an individual's name or changes the individual's postal address. Impersonation of the deceased: A fraudster uses the identity of a deceased person to obtain goods and/or services. **Phishing:** A fraudster sends an e-mail to an individual claiming to be from his or her bank or other legitimate online business (e.g., a shop or auction website) asking the individual to update or confirm his or her personal or financial information, such as password and account details. This information is then used to impersonate the targeted individual and gain access to accounts. **Present (Current) Address Fraud:** A fraudster living at your address (e.g., a family member) or nearby (e.g., a person living in the same block of flats) uses your name to purchase goods and/or services and intercepts the mail when it arrives.

Case Study 1.1   A Comparative Case of the UK Fraud Advisory
Panel, CIFAS and IdentityForce on the Categories of Internal
Information Theft

The categories of internal information theft depend on the various
intentions of the perpetrators. Some of the intentions are deliberate
with malicious intent; inappropriate and not malicious intent; and
unintentional without malice. Verizon DBIR (2013) agreed with the
UK Fraud Advisory Panel (2011) and indicated that 93 per cent of
internal information thefts were linked to deliberate malicious activity. This report noted that some interconnected intentions drive 'the
inappropriate' and not malicious intent, and unintentional without
malice. Under the category of those perpetrators with malicious intention, three-quarters of them had authorised access to the information
stolen, with approximately 19 per cent of the cases involving either
collusion or collaboration with outside accomplices.

In contrast, the CIFAS Report (2011) has earlier claimed that that
internal information criminal might have had different intentions.
CIFAS reports that 35 per cent of the perpetrators stole from their
employers to gain a new job, of which 25 per cent of these perpetrators gave the stolen assets to the new companies. In addition, IdentityForce (2014) claims that in 25 per cent of internal information
theft-related crimes, the perpetrators were actively recruited by someone outside the targeted company, of which 65 per cent were coerced
at their workplace, 15 per cent were coerced remotely while accessing
their employers' networks from their homes or other location, and
more than 25 per cent of the coercion location remained unknown.

1.9. IMPACTS OF INTERNAL INFORMATION THEFT IN THE RETAIL BUSINESS

This section answers the question of why you should be bothered with prevention of internal information theft. It looks at the socio-economic costs of
internal information theft in retail business. The discussion in this section is
based on research findings and business case studies and reports. The evolution of e-businesses has left their customers vulnerable to internal information theft-related crimes, which leave countless victims in their wake,
including online retail companies. In the 1990s, when the first third-party
services—First Virtual, Cybercash, and Verisign—for e-business transactions were introduced, Greenberg and Barling (1996) noted that about 62
per cent of employees perpetrated information theft in e-businesses. Recent
studies hold that internal information theft is on the rise (Skolov, 2005)

and that as many as 70 per cent of information thefts are committed in the workplace (Collins, 2006). CIFAS (2013) suggests that the socio-economic costs of information theft to retail businesses are inestimable. Due to increasing incidents of internal information theft-related crimes across world regions and business sectors, it is arguably difficult to record actual socio-economic costs. The costs range from irreparable brand damage to psychological damage to the victims, to name but two.

1.9.1.   Internal Information Theft: A Global Retail Business Issue

Cases of internal information theft in businesses across the world have not decreased in the past decades. KPMG, Kroll and CIFAS Joint Survey suggest that information theft and employees' fraud-related losses cost more than $1.4 million per one billion US dollars of sales (Kroll Global Fraud Report, 2013).

This survey indicates that information theft and internal financial fraud are top rated irrespective of the world regions, except in the Pacific East, where intellectual property (IP) counterfeiting and collusion are of high percentages. This is in line with the findings of the Association of Certified Fraud Examiners (ACFE), cited in Wells (2010), which suggest that a majority of businesses lost 5 per cent of their annual revenue to information theft—which accounts for more than 80 per cent of 1, 900 cases of employee's fraud. Identity Theft Resource Centre (2008) reports that internal information theft costs businesses across the world about $221 billion annually, with businesses in the UK and the United States losing over £3.2 billion and $50 billion respectively per annum.

In Canada, information theft is rated the fastest growing among other crimes (Cavoukian, 2013; Hille et al., 2015). In Australia, the cost is estimated to be more than $3 billion, of which businesses losses accounted for between AUD$1 billion and AUD$4 billion (Queensland Police Service Police (QPS) Major Fraud Investigative Group, 2009). The Queensland Audit Office attributed this cost to the muddled attitude of the most top business managers, who generally believe that information theft-related crimes are principally carried out online by hackers and their collaborators (Walliker, 2006; Passmore, 2009; Prosch, 2009). In contrast to the Australian case of information theft, the Organised Crime Strategy Report (OCSR) (2005–2009) suggests that more than 80 per cent of the senior executives admitted that they have been hit by several cases of information theft-related crimes. From this OCSR's survey, information theft cases accounted for the record loss by surpassing any kind of staff fraud for the first time in four year of OCSR's survey history. This report further notes that 48 per cent of these top business executives agreed that risks of information theft dissuaded their contemporary retail business entries across the world. Potter and Waterfall (2012) suggest that many business leaders have spent more than £38 billion as part of global cyber security strategies for the prevention of information theft.

Case Study 1.2   Impact of Internal information Theft on UK Retail Businesses

The UK National Audit Office Report (2013) on cyber security strategy suggests that cybercrime costs more than £27 billion per annum with the majority of this cost (£21billion) attributed to information theft from UK businesses. National Fraud Authority (NFA) Report (2013), which uses systematic research techniques to analyse employee-related fraud, has estimated that fraud loss against UK businesses is more than £73 billion per annum. In this report, identity theft-related crimes accounted for 14.1 per cent, while 31.3 per cent of this loss is associated with internal information theft.

Based on the UK's Staff Fraudscape by Hurst (2010), which estimated the cost of internal information theft in UK businesses to be £3.2 billion, it can be arguably concluded that the cost of information theft to UK businesses has increased by sevenfold since 2010. In as much as the costs for information theft are on the rise, so are the numbers of victims. Kroll Global Fraud Report (2013) indicates that 48 per cent of businesses in the UK are victims of information theft. This report agrees with the CIFAS: Fraud Prevention Fraud Service (2012) that the UK is second to Iceland with the highest cases of internal information theft amongst 25 nations, which in turn supports Hub International's (2010) report that internal information theft has become one of the fastest growing types of employee fraud in the UK. CIFAS (2012) indicates that there is a more than 50 per cent rise in the number of cases of information theft compared to previous years, which account for as much as 80 per cent of all computer and Internet related crimes.

Identity Theft Resource Centre (ITRC) (2008) noted that lack of reliable guides and research resources on information theft-related crimes have been the major challenges of, and may continue to inhibit research into, possible intervention strategies. ITRC's *Identity Theft: The Aftermath* (2005–2008) has consistently argued that business stakeholders in some cases declined to report internal information theft cases to law enforcement in order to protect the name of their organisation. This argument was supported by Dean et al. (2012) in their interview of 850 senior-level executives to examine the impact of internal information theft on their companies' brand names. Dean et al. (2012) found that for business brands with a worth between $1 million and $10 billion, the average minimum loss associated with information theft was worth 12 per cent of their brand value. This report supports the argument of ITRC (2008) in relation to the reason that some business managers refuse to admit the scale of internal information theft-related crimes.

They tend to protect their jobs and their business brand's name from potential reputational damage. IBM Research agrees with this argument that business managers protect their reputation and reported that 73 per cent of IS employees fear losing their job if there is reported case of internal information theft in their companies (Chen and Rohatgi, 2008).

1.9.2. Internal Information Theft: A Case of Online Retail Companies

It is not uncommon to report a continuous rise in the cost of information theft in the online retail sector. Kroll Global Fraud Report (2013) identified online retail as one of e-business sectors where the incidents of internal information theft-related crimes are prevalent. In line with Kroll's (2013) report, the BRC (2013) survey indicates that retail fraud has increased, with internal information theft on the rise and that one in three consumers do not shop online because of perceived online retail information security loopholes.

Case Study 1.3   The Cost of Information Theft to UK Retail Business

The British Retail Consortium (BRC, 2015) estimates the cost of electronic crimes (including internal identity theft-related crimes) to the retail sector by surveying UK retailers that, it stated, were responsible for 45 per cent of online UK retail sales. BRC estimated total losses of over £603 million to retail crime in 2013–2014. BRC also estimated total losses of over £205 million in 2011–2012. These estimates largely focused on losses from internal identity theft-related crimes and e-commerce frauds, as retailers were unable to estimate losses from cyber-dependent crimes.

Levels of crimes increased by 12 per cent in 2013–2014, with 135,814 incidents reported during the year, accounting for 37 per cent of the total £603 million cost of retail crime. The total cost comprised £77.3 million in direct losses (e.g., identification-related frauds, card and card-not-present (CNP) frauds and refund frauds), £16.5 million in security costs and £111.6 million in lost revenue from fraud prevention (caused by online retail security measures, such as driving away legitimate purchases). At the same time, the level of in-store theft has risen in 2013–2014 with an average of £241 per cent, 36 per cent up from the same time the previous year. These estimates bring the direct cost of retail crime to 3 million offences against UK retails during 2013–2014.

These findings agree with Shah et al. (2013) that issues of privacy related to security concerns are a major challenge for retail companies. These security issues in retail businesses have geared up the increasing cost of information theft, which has not decreased for a decade. For instance, in the case of UK retail companies, the cases of information theft have continued to rise in more than a decade. In 2004, the estimated cost of information theft to UK retailers was estimated at £498 million, which is double the £282 million estimated in 2003 (CIFAS: Staff Fraud Report, 2012), outweighing other business sectors by comparison.

The above reports and case studies support Stickley's (2009) suggestion that cases of information theft are considerably greater in number in online retail than in other business sectors due to the modes of its business operation. In contrast to the causes of rising information theft cases that have been linked to retail business operation by Stickley (2009), the CIFAS Fraud Report (2011) noted that 76 per cent of retailers agreed that the increase of information theft incidents might be linked to recent economic crises. This report revealed that there is an increase of 19.86 per cent of information theft cases in 2010 compared with the figures from the first quarter of 2009. This report suggests that more than 70 per cent of internal information thefts accounted for the total number of computer-related frauds committed. This report also corresponds to Gill's (2011) suggestions that the tendency of employees to engage in information theft-related crimes is due to the current adverse global economic climate.

The impacts of information theft losses and damage are inestimable. In some cases, businesses were unable to recover the cost of the damage, especially smaller businesses like online retailing, where internal information theft-related crimes discourage emerging smaller retailers from going into e-commerce (Yuan, 2005).

Case Study 1.4   Information Theft Incident Prediction for 2015– 2016 in the UK

Some of the 30 per cent of retailers questioned by BRC suggest that internal information theft-related crimes, including cyber-enabled fraud, will be the most significant information security-related threats in 2014–2015 and 2015–2016. This prediction suggests that theft by staff would increase by 10 per cent, theft of customers' details (15 per cent) and theft by customers (18 per cent). However, this research concludes that it might be difficult to estimate such losses accurately because of possible inevitable overlap of reports. Some of the survey-based estimates (e.g., Financial Fraud Action, BRC) that have been undertaken to date are likely to represent just a fraction of the individuals/retail companies surveyed. In addition, the estimated losses might be skewed upwards by extreme losses reported by a few respondents for business interests.

For instance, Financial Fraud Action UK (2014, p. 14) indicated that: "Online fraud against UK retailers totalled an estimated £105.5 million in 2013, a rise of 4 per cent on the previous year. However, there has been a substantial increase in fraud against online retailers based overseas, rising 48 per cent to an estimated £57.8 million". This estimate of losses reported by Financial Fraud Action UK relates to just the retail sector and not the banks/payments industry, or the public. Financial Fraud Action uses only Internet-enabled CNP fraud as a measure of 'ecommerce fraud', but Home Office (2013) suggests that a more comprehensive report of loss estimated for the cases of internal information theft and e-commerce frauds should also include other digital payments systems, such as those from PayPal.

Other impacts reported by Kroll (2013) include outraged customers, soured B2B relationships, decrease in corporate earnings, loss of investor confidence, job losses, legal settlements, psychological issues to victims, business disruption and governmental scrutiny. Sometimes, these impacts extend to businesses (banking industry) that provide payment cards to retail customers. Reflecting on these case studies, one may expect retail companies to sack hundreds of their employees every year. But sacking the employees might not be the better option to solve internal information theft problems. Thus, the insights into these impacts of information theft cases make it very important to offer a strategic and effective prevention guide for online retail businesses.

1.10. SUMMARY OF CHAPTER 1

This chapter has provided a contextual understanding of internal information theft in retail business. It has answered some contextual questions of what information theft means in the retail businesses by citing some recent research and reports. Some theories in the domain of the workplace and in criminology were used to analyse the motives of internal information theft perpetrators. The analyses were extended to the knowledge of methods and opportunities used by the perpetrators. The explanation of the resulting fraud practices related to internal information theft was also provided. In addition, this chapter has provided an overview of the impacts of internal information theft by looking into case studies and reports in retail companies. The next step in this guide is about getting to know the characteristics of information theft perpetrators. Chapter 2 looks into the characteristics of perpetrators in relation to the nature of the information theft they committed, their motivation, age (at the time of the theft), gender, job title, how they were caught and lessons learnt.

NOTES

1 The Anti-Phishing Working Group founded in 2003 is an international consortium of organisations (including BitDefender, Symantec, McAfee, VeriSign, VISA, IronKey, Mastercard, Internet Identity, ING Group, etc.) affected by phishing attacks (http://www.antiphishing.org)
2 Personal Identifiable Data

REFERENCES

Ahuja, V. (1997). *Secure Commerce on the Internet.* New York: Academic Press.

Anti-Phishing Working Group (APWG). (2014). 'Phishing activity trends report: Unifying the global response to cybercrime, 1st Quarter, 2014'. Available: http://docs.apwg.org/reports/apwg_trends_report_q1_2014.pdf, Accessed 10 June 2014.

Association of Certified Fraud Examiners (ACFE). (2014). 'Report to the nations on occupational fraud and abuse: Global fraud study'. Available: http://www.acfe.com/rttn/docs/2014-report-to-nations.pdf, Accessed 20 April 2014.

Black, D. (1987). 'The elementary forms of conflict management', Lecture Series, School of Justice Studies, Arizona State University, Tempe, Arizona.

British Retail Consortium (BRC). (2013). 'Retail crime survey'. Available: http://www.brc.org.uk/ePublications/BRC_Retail_Crime_Survey_2013/, Accessed 10 April 2014.

British Retail Consortium (BRC). (2015). BRC Retail Crime Survey 2014, Available: http://www.sbrcentre.co.uk/images/site_images/14591_BRC_Retail_Crime_Survey_2014.pdf, Accessed 19/04/2015.

Brooks, P. and Kamp, J. (1991). 'Perceived organisational climate and employee, Counter-productivity'. *Journal of Business and Psychology*, 5(4), pp. 447–458.

Burke, P.J. (2008). ' "Identity control theory", In: H.P. Clemens (Ed.), "Blackwell Encyclopaedia of Sociology" '. *Reference Reviews*, 22(3), pp. 18–18.

Cast, A. (2003). 'Identities and behaviour'. In: P. Burke, T. Owens, R. Serpe, and P. Thoits (Eds.), *Advances in Identity Theory and Research.* New York: Kluwer, pp. 42–53.

Cavoukian, A. (2013). 'Privacy by design and the promise of SmartData'. In: Inman Harvey, Ann Cavoukian, George Tomko, Don Borrett, Hon Kwan, Dimitrios Hatzinakos (Eds.), *Smart Data in Privacy Meets 1375 Evolutionary* Robotics. New York: Springer, pp. 1–9.

Checkpoint. (2013). 'Security report'. Available: http://sc1.checkpoint.com/documents /securityreport/files/assets/common/downloads/publication.pdf, Accessed 12 May 2013, pp. 4–49.

Chen, P. and Rohatgi, P. (2008). 'IT security as risk management: A research perspective'. IBM Research Report, Thomas J. Watson Research Centre, Yorktown Heights, New York.

CIFAS: The UK's Fraud Prevention Service. (2011). 'Fraud trends: Fraud level surge upwards'. Available: http://www.cifas.org.uk/annualfraudtrends-jantwelve, Accessed 26 August 2013.

CIFAS: The UK's Fraud Prevention Service. (2012). 'Staff fraudscape: Depicting the UK's staff fraud Landscape'. Available: https://www.cifas.org.uk/secure/content PORT/uploads/documents/External-0-StaffFraudscape_2012.pdf

CIFAS: The UK's Fraud Prevention Service. (2013). 'The true cost of insider fraud, Centre for Counter Fraud Studies', pp. 1–11. Available: https://www.cifas.org.uk/secure/contentPORT/uploads/documents/External-CIFAS-The-True-Cost-of-Internal-Fraud.pdf, Accessed 4 January 2014.

Clarke, E. (2009). 'How secure is your client data? 5 questions you should ask your IT professionals'. *Journal of Financial Planning*, pp. 24–25.

Clarke, R.V. (1999). *Hot Products: Understanding, Anticipating and Reducing the Demand for Stolen Goods, Police Research Series, 98*. London: Home Office.

Collins J. M. (2006). *Preventing Identity Theft in Your Business*. Hoboken, NJ: John Wiley and Sons Inc., pp. 1–256.

Cressey, R.D. (1973). 'Other people's money: A study in the social psychology of embezzlement'. *International Review of Modern Sociology*, 3(1), pp. 114–116.

CSO Magazine. (2011). 'Most computer related fraud is an inside job, says survey'. Available: http://www.csoonline.com/article/693649/most-fraud-is-an-inside-job-says-survey, Accessed 23 September 2011.

Davis, E.S. (2003). 'A world wide problem on the world wide web: International responses to transnational identity theft via the Internet'. *Journal of Law and Policy*, 12(1), pp. 201–227.

Dean, S., Pett, J., Holcomb, C., Roath, D. and Sharm, N. (2012). 'Fortifying your defences: The role of internal audit in assuring data security and privacy'. PCW Publications. Available: http://www.PWC.com/us/en/risk-assurance-services/pub lications/internal-audit-assuring-data-security-privacy.jhtml, Accessed 9 October 2012.

Denning, D.E. and William, E.B. (2000). *Hiding Crimes in Cyberspace*. London: Routledge.

Ditton, J. (1977). *Part-Time Crime: An Ethnography of Fiddling and Pilferage*. London: Macmillan.

Douglas, M. (1970). *Natural Symbols: Explanations in Cosmology*. Harmsworth: Penguin.

Duffin, M., Keats, G. and Gill, M. (2006). *Identity Theft in the UK: Offender and Victim Perspective*. Leicester: Perpetuity Research and Consultancy International Ltd.

Fighting Retail Crime Report. (2012). Available: http://www.adderdigitalcc.tv/downloads /EmployeeTheft.pdf, Accessed 20 April 2013.

Financial Fraud Action UK. (2014). 'Fraud the facts 2014: The definitive overview of payment industry fraud and measures to prevent it'. Available: http://www.financialfraudaction.org.uk/download.asp?file=2796.

Forrsights Report. (2013). 'Workforce employee survey'. Available: http://www.free movealliance.com/wp-content/uploads/2013/06/Orange-Enterprise-Mobililty.pdf, Accessed 1 October 2013.

FraudTrack. (2012). 'FraudTrack 9: Under starters order'. Available: http://www.ibe.org.uk/userimages/bdofraudtrack9.pdf, Accessed 12 December 2013.

Gerring, J. (2001). *Social Science Methodology: A Critical Framework*. Cambridge: Cambridge University Press.

Gill, M. (2011). 'Fraud and recessions: Views from fraudsters and fraud managers'. *International Journal of Law, Crime and Justice*, 39(3), pp. 204–214.

Goffman, E. (1990). *Stigma: Notes on the Management of Spoiled Identity*. London: Penguin.

Greenberg, L. and Barling, J. (1996). 'Employee theft'. *Journal of Organisational Behaviour*, 3, pp. 46–64.

Green-King, T. (2011). 'Social engineering hits 42% businesses in UK'. Available: http://www.spamfighter.com/News-16838-Social-Engineering-Hit-42-Businesses-in UK.htm, Accessed 30 September 2012.

Hille, P., Walsh, G. and Cleveland, M. (2015). 'Consumer fear of online identity theft: Scale development and validation'. *Journal of Interactive Marketing*, 30(2015), pp. 1–19.

Hinds, J. (2007). *Tackling Staff Fraud and Dishonesty: Managing and Mitigating the Risks*. London: Chartered Institute of Personnel and Development Guide.

H M Cabinet Office. (2002). *Identity Fraud: A Study*. London: Cabinet Office.

Hollinger, R.D. (1997). *Crime, Deviance and the Computer*. Aldershot, UK: Dartmouth.

Home Office. (2011). "A new approach to crimes, policy report". Policy Report—Helping the police fight crime more effectively, pp. 3–12.

Home Office. (2013). 'Cybercrime: A review of the evidence-Summary of key findings and implications'. Home Office Research Report 75, pp. 4–20.

Home Office Identity Fraud Steering Committee. (2006). Updated estimate of cost of identity fraud to UK economy. Available at: http://www.identitytheft.org.uk/ID%20fraud%20table.pdf> Accessed 14 July 2013.

Hub International. (2010). 'Identity theft in the information age: Protecting your most valued asset'. White Paper, pp. 1–12.

Hurst, P. (2010). *Staff Fraudscape: Depicting the United Kingdom's Staff Fraud Land Scape*. London: CIFAS.

Identity Theft Resource Centre (ITRC). (2008). 'Identity Theft: The Aftermath 2007'. Available: http://harvardbenefits.com/downloads/Group%20Sales%20Docs/Identity%20Theft%20The%20Aftermath%202007%20Report.pdf

IdentityForce Report. (2014). *Identity Theft Protection with Identity Force*. Available: http://www.asecurelife.com/identity-force/, Accessed 12 July 2014.

James, B. (2006). 'Review of the legal status and rights of victims of identity theft in Australasia'. *Australasian Centre for Policing Research, Report Series*, 142(2), pp. 1–6.

Johns, G. (1987). 'The great escape'. *Psychology Today*, 21, pp. 30–33.

Josselson, R., McAdams, D. and Lieblich, A. (2006). 'Introduction'. In: D. McAdams R. Josselson and A. Lieblich (Eds.), *Identity and Story: Creating Self in Story*. Washington, DC: American Psychological Association, pp. 3–11.

Kantor, S. (1983). 'How to foil employee crime'. *Nation's Business* (July), pp. 38–39.

Kardell, R.L. (2007). 'Three steps to fraud prevention in the workplace'. ACFE Report to the Nation of Occupational Fraud and Abuse, pp. 16–19.

Koops, B. J., Leenes, R., Meints, M., van der Meulen, N. and Jaquet-Chifelle, D. (2009). 'A typology of identity-related crime: Conceptual, technical, and legal issues'. *Information, Communication and Society*, 12(1), pp. 1–24.

Kroll Global Fraud Report. (2013). *Who's got something to hide? Searching for Insider Fraud.* Available: http://fraud.kroll.com/wp-content/uploads/2013/10/FraudReport_2011–2012.pdf, Accessed 8 February 2013.

Lacoste, J. and Tremblay, P. (2003). 'Crime innovation: A script analysis of patterns in check forgery'. *Crime Prevention Studies*, 16, pp. 171–198.

Leslie, C. and Hood, A., (2009). *Circling the Loan Sharks: Predatory Lending in the Recession and the Emerging Role for Local Government.* London: New Local Government Network.

Mars, G. (1974). 'Dock pilferage: A case study in occupational theft'. In: P. Rock and M. McIntosh (Eds.), *Deviance and Social Control.* London: Tavistock, pp. 209–228.

Mars, G. (1982). *Cheats at Work: Anthropology of Workplace Crime.* London: Allen and Unwin.

Mars, G. (Ed.) (2001). *Sabotage.* Aldershot, UK: Ashgate.

Mars, G. (2006). 'Changes in occupational deviance: Scams, fiddles and sabotage in the twenty-first century'. *Crime, Law and Social Change*, 2006(45), pp. 285–296.

Meulen, N. (2011). 'Financial identity theft: Context, challenges and countermeasure'. *Information Technology and Law Series*, 22, pp. 25–36.

Mitnick, K.D. and Simon, W.L. (2006). *The Art of the Intrusion: Real Stories Behind the Exploits of Hackers, Intruders and Deceivers.* New York: Wiley Publishing Inc.

Morris II, R.G. (2004). 'The development of an identity theft offender typology: A theoretical approach'. Available: http://www.shsu.edu/~edu_elc/ journal/research% 20online/re2004/Robert.pdf, Accessed 23 August 2011.

MPS Operation Sterling. (2009). 'Fraud prevention advice'. Available: http://content.met.police.uk/cs/Satellite?blobcol=urldata&blobheadername1=Content-Type&blobheadername2=Content_Disposition&blobheadervalue1=application%2Fpdf&blobheadervalue2=inline%3B+filename%3D%22429%2F88%2Foperation_sterling_fraud_prevention_advice%2C0.pdf%22&blobkey=id&blobtable=MungoBlobs&blobwhere=1283598280241&ssbinary=true, Accessed 23 June 2013.

National Fraud Authority Report. (2013). *Annual Fraud Indicator.* London: NFA, pp. 7–32.

Newman, G.R. (2004). 'Identity theft, problem-oriented guides for police'. Problem-Specific Guides Series, No. 25, U.S. Department of Justice.

Newman, G. and Clarke, R. (2003). *Superhighway Robbery: Preventing E-Commerce Crime.* London: Willan.

Organisation for Economic Cooperation and Development (OECD). (2008). 'Policy guidance on online identity theft'. OECD Ministerial Meeting on the future of the Internet Economy Seoul.

Organised Crime Strategy Report. (2005–2009). Available: www.police.vic.gov.au/retrievemedia.asp?Media_ID=2544, Accessed 04 June 2012.

Passmore, D. (2009). 'Sunshine state is hacker's paradise'. *The Sunday Mail, Brisbane Queensland.* Available: http://www.news.com.au/news/sunshine-state-is-a-hackers-paradise/story-fna7dq6e-1225745965102, Accessed 17 October 2011.

Peretti, K.K. (2009). 'Data breaches: What the underground work of 'carding' reveals'. *Sanat Clara Computer and High-Technology Law Journal*, 25(2), pp. 375–413.

Perl, M.W. (2003). 'It's not always about the money: Why the state identity theft laws fail to adequately address criminal record identity theft'. *Journal of Criminal Law and Criminology*, **94**(1), pp. 169–208.

Potter, C. and Waterfall, G. (2012). 'PriceWaterCoopers' Information security breaches survey: Technical Report'. Available: www.infosec.co.uk, Accessed on 15 October 2012.

Prosch, M. (2009). 'Preventing identity theft throughout the data life cycle'. *Journal of Accountancy*, **207**(1), pp. 58–62.

Queensland Police Service (QPS) Major Fraud Investigative Group. (2009). 'Theft by fraud. Queensland police service'. *Police Bulletin*, pp. 27–30.

Raab, C.D. (2008). 'Social and political dimensions of identity'. In: S. Fischer-Hübner, P. Duquenoy, A. Zuccato and L. Martucci (Eds.), *The Future of Identity in the Information Society*. New York: Springer, pp. 3–19.

Savage, M. (2003). 'Former hacker Mitnick details the threat of social engineering.' CRN, no.1043, April, 2003, p. 58.

Shah, M.H., Okeke, R.I. and Ahmed, R. (2013). 'Issues of privacy and trust in E-commerce: Exploring customers' perspectives'. *Journal of Basic and Applied Scientific Research*, **3**(3), pp. 571–577.

Shearman, C. and Burrell, G. (1988). 'New technology base firms and the emergence of new industries: Some employment implications'. *New Technology, Work and Employment*, **3**(2), pp. 87–99.

Sokolov, A.P. (2005). *Identity Theft on the Rise*. Hauppauge, NY: Nova Science Publishers Inc.

Stickley, J. (2009). *The Truth About Identity Theft. Why Be Me When I Can Be You?* Upper Saddle River, NJ: Pearson Education.

Sutton, A., Cherney, A. and White, R. (2013). *Crime Prevention: Principles, Perspective and Practices*. Cambridge: Cambridge University Press, pp. 1–276.

Thompson, P. and McHugh, D. (2009). *Work Organisations: A Critical Approach* (2nd edn.). Chippenham and Eastbourne: Palgrave Macmillan.

Tucker, J. (1989). 'Employee theft as a social control'. *Journal of Deviant Behaviour*, **10**(4), pp. 319–334.

UK Fraud Advisory Panel. (2011). 'Fraud facts, information for individuals' (2nd edn). 1, pp. 1–2. Available: https://www.fraudadvisorypanel.org/wp-content/uploads/2015/04/Fraud-Facts-1I-Identity-Fraud-Revised-Sep11.pdf, Issue 1 September 2011 (2nd edition).

UK National Audit Office Report. (2013). 'Cost of cybercrime (2013)'. Available: https://www.gov.uk/goverment/uploads/system/uploads/attachment_data/file/60943/the-cost-of-cyber-crime-full-report.pdf.

Verizon. (2013). 'Data breach investigation report'. Available: http://www.verizonenterprise.com/resources/reports/dbir-series-why-businesses-are-attacked_en_xg.pdf, Accessed 27 December 2013.

Verizon RISK Team Survey Report. (2012). 'Data breach investigations report'. Available: http://www.verizonbusiness.com/resources/reports/rp_data-breach-investigations-report2012_en_xg.pdf, Accessed 23 April 2013.

Walliker, A. (2006). 'Identity theft soars and now costs $3 billion a year', *Sunday Hearld-Sun. Melbourne Victoria*, p. 88.

Wells, J. (2010). 'ACFE report'. *Journal of Accountancy*, **177**, pp. 1–82.

Wortley, R. (1997). *Reconsidering the Role of Opportunity in Situational Crime Prevention.* Dartmouth, UK: Ashgate, pp. 65–81.

Yeager, P.C. (2007). 'Understanding corporate law breaking: from profit seeking to law finding'. In: H. Pontell and G. Geis (Eds.), *International Handbook of White-Collar Crime.* New York: Springer, pp. 25–49.

Yuan, L. (2005). 'Companies face system attacks from inside, too'. *The Wall Street Journal Online.*

2 Know the Nature of Internal Information Theft

2.1. INTRODUCTION

This chapter provides behind the scenes analysis of cases of internal information theft, in most cases within a retail environment, revealing what went wrong and illustrating how the theft was perpetrated, even the most unsuspecting operation. It provides in-depth understanding of the characteristics of information theft perpetrators in the targeted retail companies. This analysis is essential for readers to have a comprehensive knowledge of real time data of where and how the perpetrators operate. Haley (2013) suggests that if information security experts or crime prevention practitioners do not know how perpetrators exploit retail companies' risks and vulnerabilities, they may not have adequate knowledge to develop and implement a security strategy. Adhering to this suggestion, this chapter introduces a number of examples of individuals who have been caught attempting or engaging in internal information theft.

The majority of the cases analysed in this chapter were extracted from the public archives of the UK Association of Business Crime Partnerships and UK National Fraud Authority. Case analysis of internal information theft perpetrators covers their age (at the time of the fraud), gender, job title, description of the nature of the fraud (attempt), motivation, how they were caught and lessons learnt. Some of the cases of corporate information theft analysed were collected from the public domain. In those cases, the names of the fraudsters were retained. In the cases that were not in the public domain, no identifying information is given and all the names have been changed to protect the individuals' privacy. The internal information thefts analysed here have been categorised under corporate information theft.

Although full discussion of these categories has been discussed in the section 1.1.4.3 of Chapter 1, it is important to revisit those explanations in this chapter to provide comprehensive understanding of the perpetrators' characteristics.

Case Study 2.1   Record Rise in the Cases of Information Theft in the UK (UK's ONS, 2014)

The number of internal information theft cases recorded by fraud prevention bodies and law enforcement agencies had risen by nearly by 60 per cent in five years in England and Wales. According to the Office of National Statistics (ONS) (2014), more than 230,000 cases of internal information theft-related crimes/frauds were recorded in England and Wales from January to June 2014. This figure represents a 59 per cent rise in five years and more than a fifth on the previous 12 months. Online retail and banking sectors recorded a further 316,000 cases of related employees frauds. In total, over 12 million cases of information theft and related employee fraud were recorded in the 12-month period.

However, the ONS (2014) noted that these figures recorded across business sectors may have overlapped. These reports suggest the prevalent nature of information theft in UK e-business sectors. The rise in these crimes in both retail and banking sectors may have been due to the nature of the online business operation of these sectors, which carry less risk of being caught. Norman Baker, the UK's minister of state in the coalition government of 2013–2014, and Jack Dromey, the UK shadow policing minister, noted that information theft-related fraud has increased by 21 per cent because much of these online crimes go unreported.

2.2. INTERNAL INFORMATION THEFT PERPETRATION METHODS

The common methods include unauthorised alteration to company data/modification of company payment instructions. In some cases, the fraudsters who have stolen financial information use it for money laundering or services by deception. This often involves the use of counterfeit or forged companies' documents. The common schemes include Application Fraud/Account Takeover, Present (Current) Address Fraud and Account Withdrawal. They also involve the compromise of information systems, network, data, which identify the victim as the statutory owner under the UK Data Protection Act, 1998. The victims in this case are the retail companies in relation to their customer. The theft involves acts where the suspect/perpetrator has used their legitimate access to IS and network to perpetrate internal information theft. The suspect/perpetrators include current/former employees of the victim retail companies, current/former consultant/contractor/partners.

The case of the individuals analysed are not limited to the UK online retail sector. It has included some cases of other sectors (e.g., banking) because of the multifaceted operational nature of the retail sector business through credit/debit cards. These cases were directly or indirectly involved with online retail and banking sectors due to the relationships both sectors share in their business operations.

Companies allow consumers to buy goods or services from a seller using various web browsers and portals, which include the use of business-to-business (B2B) online shopping and processing of services. During the retail transaction, retail companies subcontract to or collaborate with banks in processing consumer card information and authorising the payment for the complete online shopping operation.

Table 2.1   Case of Internal Information Theft: Account Takeover

Name	'Jane'
Age	32
Gender	Female
Job title	Cashier
Nature	'Jane' stole numerous credit cards that were left by customers in a rush after shopping. She used the cards to make purchases from her own company's online portal. After several weeks, when the crime was not discovered, she continued to use the debit cards to make more purchases from other online retail portals.
Motivation	**Opportunity:** She had an opportunity and she took it. She believed that everyone in the shop could have done the same.**Self-Justification:** 'Jane's' main justification was that she didn't think she was doing something wrong. She had the opportunity and made use of it. She thought that everyone would have done the same and that could justify her fraud as the norm.**Absence monitoring system like CCTV cameras:** Because there is no monitoring/surveillance in place to check the employees' internal shop activities, 'Jane' was convinced that she would never be caught.
How caught	One customer whose credit card 'Jane' had stolen came in the next day after she had realised that she had left her card behind, checked with her bank and found out it had already been used. 'Jane's' company called the police and she got arrested.

Case Study 2.2   Lessons Learnt from Case of an Account Takeover

Perpetrators' perception of lack of effective security: Due to 'Jane's' company's lack of verification procedures, she found it easy to bypass their website defences. It was easy for her to defraud e-commerce sites that have no identity verification or shared fraud alert data, which could have been used to trail and alert others to her dubious purchases. If there were identity checks such as name and address, a more complete identification of the individual could have emerged which would flag negative fraud alerts in the customer databases.

   Failure of the credit card companies to report the fraud: It was easy for Jane to continue her fraudulent scheme because the credit card companies failed to report the fraud to the card owner.

   Customer Negligence: In addition, there was negligence on the part of most online retail customers to check their spending regularly with their banks.

Table 2.2   Case of Internal Information Theft from Database

Name	'Smith'
Age	24
Gender	Male
Job title	Software Engineer
Nature	'Smith' gathered customers' personal identifiable information from his Company's information systems and sold them on the 'black market'.
Motivation	Expertise: 'Smith' has used his technical skills to exploit the information systems of his employer and stole information for his personal gains. The Demand for Personal Information by Fraudsters: The huge demand for the online credit/debit card details has created a 'hot product' perception for both 'Smith' and his customers.
How Caught	'Smith's' hacking activities on the information systems were revealed by the biannual information audit. The trails of how he logged into the company's information database were analysed and he was arrested. During his fraud investigation, it was revealed that numerous customers' card details were found on his personal laptop and some hidden websites that he has been using to sell the stolen card details.

Case Study 2.3   Lessons Learnt from Case of Information Theft from Database

Absence of a regular information security audit in 'Smith's' company allowed him lots of time to perpetrate internal information theft without getting caught. There is no effective security system in place to prevent 'Smith' from hacking his employer's information systems, although if it existed he would have used his IT skills to manoeuvre it. High security surveillance should have been placed on 'Smith', as he possesses software engineering skills, because he could pose a huge security threat to companies. It is import for information security managers to identify the job roles that pose the greatest internal information theft risks. Retail companies should put in place regular evaluation strategies to access the transaction trails of those in roles with high risks of vulnerabilities to internal information theft.

Table 2.3   Case of Credit Card Disclosure

Name	'Ceri'
Age	29
Gender	Female
Job title	Credit Card Issuance Officer
Nature of theft	An employee embezzled £310,698 from an employer. 'Ceri' manipulated a payroll and credit card scheme that led to her embezzling £310,698 from her small business employer over a period of five years
Motivation	Boost of Annual Salary: She was using the stolen money to boost her annual salary. Family Pressure: 'Ceri' used her employer's account to pay for her daughter's three credit card bills, totalling more than £15,000.
How Caught	Numerous calls from customers complaining about non-payment. The calls sparked an investigation that was reported to the local police. During the course of the investigation, the investigation team discovered that 'Ceri' had a record of improper use of a credit card.

Case Study 2.4   Lessons Learnt from Case of Credit Card Disclosure

Past behaviour is an excellent predictor of future behaviour. A thorough background check can provide valuable information, especially when a candidate is applying for a position of trust. Such an investigation would likely have prevented 'Ceri's' hiring. The revelation of fraudulent activities by 'Ceri' started when customers complained about not receiving their payments for services/goods rendered. This employer made a most positive move by not allowing such complaints to be investigated by the employee charged with processing those transactions.

Table 2.4   Case of Account Withdrawal

Name	'Kathy'
Age	47
Gender	Female
Job title	Accountant
Nature	An accounting clerk wrote 137 retail companies' contract payment cheques valued at £1.4 million and deposited them into her personal account. This trusted employee was given the authority to prepare cheques without proper internal safeguards and reasonable management oversight.
Motivation	**No segregation of duties/working alone:** This individual could prepare and issue cheques without being scrutinised before the cheques were authorised for payment.**Opportunity:** She had the opportunity and used it because she was 'trusted' by the government.
How Caught	This fraud scheme was actually uncovered by an accident, as result of a credit union employee calling Head of Finance and asking a question about cheques being deposited in a personal checking account. Shortly afterward it was confirmed that the account in question belonged to one of that county agency's employees. At this point, government auditors were called in and an investigative audit was launched.

Case Study 2.5   Lessons Learnt from Case of Account Withdrawal

There should be clearly defined roles and segregation duties. This would discourage the employees' ideology of 'work-alone' that allows internal information theft activities. No employee should be in a position to write company cheques or make payments without second-party confirmation that such payments are valid. 'Undue' or 'unqualified' trust causes an overwhelming number of owners and managers to fail in their jobs because they naively assume that their operation is immune from internal fraud. After all, the managers might argue that they have loyal, long-term and highly trusted employees or volunteers handling their highest-risk financial activities. A few of the managers may understand that whenever trust is incorrectly bestowed, problems are likely to follow.

2.3. FACTORS THAT ENCOURAGE INTERNAL INFORMATION THEFT

The above case studies have shown the characteristics of internal information theft perpetrators. The analysis shows that stealing of credit and debit cards details, corporate and personal account manipulation and account withdrawal are the common cases. Other research reports (e.g., CIFAS, 2012; Kroll, 2013) have shown that customers' payment card numbers and card details are the major targets. These reports suggest that corporate account details are at risk as customers' personal identifiable information (PII). Based on the lessons learnt from the above cases, the major factors for the increase in internal information theft in retail companies include:

- Lack of empirical data of internal information theft in the public domain;
- Retail business operations;
- Overdependence of security management on software security;
- Perception that internal information theft perpetrators are shop-floor employees;
- Lack of internal information theft incident analysis;
- Absence of human-centred security in online retail.

2.3.1. Lack of Empirical Data of Internal Information Theft

Readers can understand that the impacts of internal information theft are inestimable, as suggested by the examples of individuals who were caught, although indicators of the impact of information theft cases are not released to the public, possibly due to privacy-related issues, as some of the cases are in the public domain (Shah et al., 2013). Most retail companies might not be encouraged to reveal the impacts of internal information theft, as such publicity might bring some irreparable dent/damage to their companies' brand. This issue of protecting the victimised companies' brand and reputation is one of the major factors that have led to increasing cases of internal information theft in businesses (Laudise, 2008). However, without reliable data on the cases of internal information theft, it would be difficult, if not impossible, to provide a contextual preventive measure for information theft.

The case analyses above were based on the few available data in the public domain. This unavailability of data arises from three causes:

- Retail companies rarely share data on information theft incidents;
- Companies gather data on information theft incidents for narrow purposes and;
- Perpetrators always act to conceal their trails.

Internal information theft incidents data are withheld due to concern over copycat activities and publicity, and perhaps also due to privacy-related issues. Few available data were shared under guarantees of confidentiality and under restricted-use agreements.

Information theft data are available only if there is no other option. With these limited access issues, information theft data, like the ones discussed here, are rarely available to researchers. Second, retail companies have no motivation to share data related to information theft incidents. They are provided only for selected cases of forensic investigation or legal proceedings. Sometimes, the available data were not organised. In some cases, the databases were not accessible. These issues made empirical data collection, collation and analysis intensive research.

Third, most of perpetrators are skilled enough to cover their trails before the detection. In some cases, it takes short period of time to carry out successful attack. Perpetrators often devised and conceal their perpetration trails. These issues contribute to incomplete data capture on their methods of their information theft perpetration. This was noted by researchers (Newman and McNally, 2005) as one of the setbacks of information theft prevention research. However, this chapter has provided, through these case analyses, huge valuable insights despite the deficiencies in the data material.

2.3.2. Retail Business Operations

The case analysis shows that retail business operations is one of the major factors that accounts for the increasing cases of internal information theft. The case examples analysis suggest that the use of credit and debit cards through mobiles phones have encouraged successful perpetration, as most of the cases analysed directly or indirectly involve cards compromise.

In line with the discussion in Chapter 1, the case analyses suggest that desk-based employees who carry out most of the end-user online trading through credit or debit cards are more vulnerable than employees from other departments. This trend is followed by finance/accounting operation employees. These revelations suggest that most employees in retail operation are a potential threat to proprietary information because of the situational or the opportunistic nature of their job roles. This knowledge suggests that more attention should be given to the operational departments, IT departments and accounting positions, other than to age and gender. Thus, these findings suggested that the characteristics of the perpetrators are not likely to be classified based on gender but on their operational departments.

2.3.3. Overdependence of Management on Software Security

This issue of management relying too much on the software security for prevention of information theft was confirmed in the case analyses, which suggest that management of the companies leaves the activities of the employees to be monitored by security systems. This is a major issue because the information systems are designed by some of the employees; the perpetrators may be as skilled as those who designed the security software, as, for example, in the case of 'Mr. Smith', a software engineer who stole customers' card details for his financial gain. The detection capability of software security cannot match the effectiveness of the use of monitoring and security audit, as we have seen in this example of 'Mr. Smith' because he has the skills to cover his trail. The overreliance on software security can create the perception that adequate security is in place. This perception is misleading in a way that the IS security management can neglect other security measures. However, Allen et al. (1999) and Hofmeyr et al. (1998) suggest that although software security has a place for the internal information theft but cannot equate the human security—effective monitoring and security audit.

2.3.4. Perception that Perpetrators Are Shop-Floor Employees

The retail management team often see the shop-floor employees, call centre employees, as potential internal information thieves because of their operational roles in dealing with card transactions. The management often perceived themselves as the 'clean employees' that rarely indulge in information theft perpetration. This perception among security and crime prevention practitioners, as argued by Raab (2008), can cause gross negligence of the top management, who use their position to perpetrate internal information theft-related crimes. However, the knowledge drawn from the case analyses has shown that since deviance, as argued by Durkeim (1966), is 'an integral part of all healthy societies', any employee can be tempted to indulge in internal information theft if there are no effective prevention guidelines and measures in place.

2.3.5. Lack of Internal Information Theft Incident Analysis

Another notable lesson learnt from the case analyses is that some companies, apparently, have no culture of information theft incidents analysis or assessment. The detection and prosecution of perpetrators bring the incidents to a close. Case reports, in most cases, are documented for management meeting but not really for analysis and assessment. Security and crime prevention management often believe that reoccurring incidents of information theft avail them the opportunity to get experience of the intricacy of such crimes. This practice is not helpful, as an effective crime incident analysis and assessment can reduce the risks and costs of similar crimes in the future. It can also serve as a model or a clue for crime prevention management.

McLaren et al. (2011) noted that for organisations to compete in a highly dynamic security marketplace, they must frequently adapt and align their security strategies and information systems by continuous incident analysis and evaluation.

Other researchers (e.g., Lu and Ramamurthy, 2011; Ransbotham et al., 2012), have also pointed out that that security capability and empirical examination of vulnerability data disclosure mechanisms enable firms' agility against any security threats. Such strategies boost a business organisation's security proactive stance, and decrease the volume of exploitation attempts. On the contrary, the case analyses suggest that management regarded experiences as the preferred method of improving their data security and crime prevention strategies, due to the cost of hiring experts or professionals to manage either their internal data security strategies or crimes incidents analyses. As also noted by KPMG (1997), prevention of internal information theft requires effective data security risk management that can tackle the extent of the risks involved.

However, although studies suggest that it is the responsibility of management to educate employees on data security policy, and that analyses of crimes are more likely to lead to effective prevention of information theft, it is important to point out that in some incidents the case analyses are not carried out due to constraints such as finance, inadequacy of management, lack of strategy performance measures, inadequacy of management, and employees' attitudes. Ekblom (2002) and Clarke and Eck (2003) noted that availability of resources, finance and staffing are among the greatest challenges of crimes preventions within any socio-economic setting, even if clearer strategic crime prevention plans exist. Unless clearer plans are in place, management will struggle to determine priorities and areas of assistance in terms of immediate prevention action (low cost action and high risk/impact) and long-term interventions (deterrence law and penal reform, major policy changes and planning).

2.3.6. Absence of Human-Centred Security in Retail Companies

Human roles can still play a huge part in preventing internal information theft. A comprehensive discussion of human roles—the management—is presented in Chapter 3. However, the case analyses in this chapter have shown that reports from customers, law enforcement agencies and security audits are the methods through which the perpetrators were caught. These agree with the suggestions of Moore (2005) and Cappelli et al. (2006a), that the responsibilities of information theft prevention lie with human-centred security. Concerns should also be directed to employees' operational policies and monitoring of the IS security infrastructure and to the need for retail companies to invest in employee training. Researchers (e.g., Haagman and Wilkinson, 2011) suggest that employee training is one of the vital instruments for information theft prevention practice. Policy is very salient at any stage of IS security implementation; without a clear IS security policy, the IT governance of retail companies would not hold water (Leon, 2008). Sommer (2012) suggests that an effective policy implementation is the root on which other prevention.

2.4. CHARACTERISTICS OF INFORMATION THEFT PERPETRATORS

The case analysis based on the profile of the individuals caught perpetrating information theft provided a more general characterisation of and additional insights into the nature of thefts in online retail. The internal information theft cases describe variables such as age, sex and job roles that were used to characterise perpetrators, but do not presume these variables are the same for all business organisations. Retail companies need to use these identified characteristics as a reference guide to analyse internal information theft cases in their business organisation.

Based on the case examples analysed in Subchapter 2.2 above, the following major characteristics of the perpetrators can be drawn:

- *Perpetrators are not necessarily technically oriented to carry out information theft;*
- *The nature of internal information theft perpetrated by managers is comparatively different from the cases by shop-floor employees;*
- *Most internal information theft cases were detected through customer complaints, information system audits and colleagues.*

Perpetrators are not necessarily technically oriented to carry out internal information theft: This characteristic of the perpetrators suggests that the seemingly least-threatening employees—the call centre employees without technical knowledge or privileged access to retail information systems can still cause significant damage, as in Case Study 2.2 of 'Jane', who stole numerous credit cards that were left by customers in a rush after shopping. She might not have the technical capabilities of the software engineers, but she used her call-centre and operational skills to use the stolen cards to make purchases from her own company's online portal.

This finding reinforces the need that retail companies will have to adhere to good security principles across all the levels of employees, irrespective of their job roles. Hence, this study recommends that companies guide their policies and practices by restricting all levels of employees' access control. In addition, retail companies should assume that potential perpetrators will leverage exploitable IS security vulnerabilities within the research of most non-technical employees (Fichtman, 2001). And there is no amount of theft prevention systems that will defend against such perpetrators. Therefore, online retail companies can begin to minimise cases of perpetration only if they continually strengthen their policies on the principle of trusted information systems security and access control mechanisms.

The nature of information theft perpetrated by managers is comparatively different from cases by shop-floor employees: Although the business activities and access to information systems of managers and shop-floor employees may have differed at times, managers caused the damages than shop-floor employees in relation to the impact of information theft. It takes longer time to detect internal information theft penetrated by managers than those perpetrated by shop-floor employees. This finding was suggested by the case of Jessica Harper, the Head of Online Security/Lloyds Banking Group. In addition, this characteristic suggests that employees in certain job roles, such as accountants and software engineers, pose different threats different from employees in call centre positions. It behooves the companies to consider auditing the activities of employees in relation to features of their job roles. It is essential for e-businesses, including financial organisations, to develop policies and clearly enforce them for all employees with respect to their job roles and business operations but with equal disciplinary actions. Therefore, a corollary to this varying nature of information theft perpetrators is that practices should be put in place in the companies to disallow exceptional handling or the case of 'different rules for different employees'.

In addition, companies should greatly limit the amount of trust they give to employees at the management level. There should be access control that is effective enough to provide only necessary access to the employees in management positions. The case analyses suggest that employees in management positions were not closely examined or monitored by the victimised companies until it is too late. There should no case of 'sacred cow'; no employee should be monitored with preference because of their management position or because an employee makes more money for the company than other employees.

Most of the internal information theft cases were detected through customer complaints, information system audits and colleagues' suspicions: The case examples indicate that technology played a very small role in enabling the victimised companies to detect perpetrators. However, by itself this conclusion could be explained by other factors. Perhaps technological approaches could be largely successful at detecting information security flaws before more damage was done, therefore reducing the impact of the information theft, but they may not match the capability of the human roles. However, if technologically based security software had been in place, in some cases, it could have been outdated or perhaps not installed properly. In the case examples discussed above, the victim companies were very successful at detecting information theft cases by conducting audits, monitoring the employees' suspicious behaviour and questioning the employees' abnormal activities. Retail companies should establish anonymous and open communication channels to encourage their employees to report suspicious colleagues. There should be frequent impromptu and routine information security audits in place to review the operational activities of all employees. There should be a 'no exception rule', no matter the position of the employee in implementing the checks and audit processes.

2.5. SUMMARY OF CHAPTER 2

The case analyses in this chapter have reinforced the UK Fraud Bill of 2006 and UK Home Office definition, according to which information theft occurs "when sufficient information about an identity is obtained to facilitate identity crimes or fraud, irrespective of whether in the case of a person, company, organisation or an entity . . . . And this could lead to frauds of using a false identity or someone else's details for unlawful activity . . . it could be also when someone avoids falsely claiming that the criminal was the victim of identity fraud . . .; these frauds come in variety of ways and for various motives".

This could involve using a false identity or someone's personal identifiable information (PII) (e.g., name, address, date of birth) for financial/commercial gain. The perpetrators use the PII to buy goods or secure services (e.g., bank account opening for money withdrawals) or for credit cards, loan applications, and contract services.

In addition, this chapter has answered the question of what schemes or methods are used by perpetrators. From the analyses, the main techniques for stealing customer data were: copying the customers' details from the systems, diversion of the ordered products, selling of the data on the black market; organised crime—collusion, collaboration and infiltration, computer means, hacking, research of customers' identity, buying customers' data from employees with unrestricted access. In some cases, some employees pay an estate management agent to lease him a house for the purpose of collection of the redirected ordered goods from the retail companies. In similar instances, some employees reveal customer data details to an external criminal who pretends to be the real customer. And in other cases, some external criminals call into the call centre departments pretending to be from a retail company's IT department, and then ask for the customer's data or password retrieval.

The insights provided by the case analyses point to the question of the impact of internal information theft in retail companies. In particular, some retail companies' Loss Prevention team handled hundreds of cases every year. The majority of such cases reports come from call centres and from the employees handling the financial details of customers. In some cases, the Regional Loss Prevention team employees may not be comfortable to report that their work colleagues engaged in internal information theft. Consequently, the impact of the cases of internal information theft might be recorded or documented accurately.

However, the common impacts of internal information theft, among others, include: business loss, loss of customer trust, job loss, data security challenges, huge budget allocation for job recruitment, training, data security, software security, investigation costs, litigation costs, information security auditing; big challenge to the directors and management, damage to the business name, and no records of approximate company loss.

Based on the lessons from the case analyses, retail companies should direct their prevention efforts to the following measures:

- Employee training on data protection,
- Secured customers' data identification,
- Effective application and implementation of computer use policy,
- Effective implementation of IT security tools: anti-virus and firewalls, intrusion detection and penetration test,
- Restriction from the use of pen and paper and mobile phones,

In particular, employee training should be emphasised as a key internal information theft prevention strategy. Every new employee should be mandated to do online training on the Data Protection Act. The employees should also be mandated to pass the assessment that follows the training. In addition, there should be internal information theft prevention awareness and follow-up on how the training was perceived by the employees to enable the companies to evaluate the impact of employee training on the prevention of information theft.

Moreover, computer policy should be on the priority list of effective internal information prevention strategies. Companies should implement a system for a unique employee login, be ready to change access passwords regularly, forbid the downloading of applications from the Internet to the company's systems, not have access to Internet or social networking sites, not use either pen and paper or mobile phone while working (except the top managers) and employees must be compliant with password policy. There should be no exception for some managers; as such exception might lead to some leakages involving the top management.

Finally, there should be a system for secure customer data identification. A few retail companies often implement secure customer data identification as one of their strategies in prevention of internal information theft. It is necessary for companies to use and implement an intelligence system in call centres departments to confirm customers' identity. This should be built on a knowledge-based system of using identifications: either of name, address, account number, date of birth or combination of any of the personal information attributes. These systems should be designed in such a way that identification processes and questions involve some element of complexity to deter the criminal from within or from outside a company to access customers' sensitive data. However, a consequence of a knowledge-based system is that if the system fails and the company had relied upon the system for the security of the customers' data, there would be a high risk of information theft cases on such occasions. It is the responsibility of the security management to design security tools that are *well-integrated* with the retail operation to avoid risks associated with a knowledge-based system. The next discussion of this guide, in Chapter 3, looks into how the key components—people, process, and technology—can be integrated to provide an effective information theft prevention strategy.

REFERENCES

Allen, J., Christie, A., Fithen, W., McHugh, J., Pickel, J. and Stoner, E. (1999). 'State of the practice of intrusion detection technologies'. Tech. Rep. CMU/SEI-99-TR-028, Carnegie Mellon University/Software Engineering Institute, pp. 1–111.

Cappelli, D.M., Desai, A.G., Moore, A.P., Shimeall, T.J., Weaver, E.A. and Willke, B.J. (2006a). 'Management and Education of the Risk of Insider Threat (MERIT): Mitigating the risk of sabotage to employers' information, systems, or networks.' Proceedings of the 24th International System Dynamics Conference, Nijmegen, Netherlands, July.

Cappelli, D.M., Desai, A.G., Moore, A.P., Shimeall, T.J., Weaver, E.A. and Willke, B.J. (2006b). 'System dynamics modeling of computer system sabotage'. Joint CERT Coordination Center/SEI and CyLab at Carnegie Mellon University Report, Pittsburgh, PA, pp. 1–34.

CIFAS: The UK's Fraud Prevention Service. (2012). 'Staff fraudscape: Depicting the UK's staff fraud Landscape'. Available: https://www.cifas.org.uk/secure/content-PORT/uploads/documents/External-0-StaffFraudscape_2012.pdf.

Clarke, R.V., and J.E. Eck (2003). *Become a Problem-Solving Crime Analyst: In 55 Small Steps*. London: Jill Dando Institute of Crime Science.

Durkheim, E. (1966). *Suicide*. New York: Free Press.

Ekblom, P (2002) 'From the Source to the Mainstream is Uphill: The Challenge of Transferring Knowledge of Crime Prevention Through Replication, Innovation and Anticipation.' In: N. Tilley (ed.) Analysis for Crime Prevention, Crime Prevention Studies 13: 131–203. Monsey, NY: Criminal Justice Press/ Devon, UK: Willan Publishing. www.popcenter.org/Library/ CrimePrevention/Volume%2013/0 7-Ekblom.pdf

Fichtman, P. (2001). 'Preventing credit card fraud and identity theft: A primer for online merchants'. *Information Systems Security*, 10(5), pp. 1–8.

Haagman, D. and Wilkinson, S. (2011). 'Good Practice Guide for Computer-Based Electronic Evidence'. Association of Chief Police Officer (ACPO): 7Safe Information Security, Official Release, pp. 6–72.

Haley, C. (2013). 'A theory of cyber deterrence'. *Georgetown Journal of International Affairs*. Available: http://Journal.Georgetown.Edu/A-Theory-Of-Cyber-Deterrence-Christopher-Haley, Accessed 23 April 2014.

Hofmeyr, S.A., Forrest, S. and Somayaji, A. (1998). 'Intrusion detection using sequences of systems calls'. *Journal of Computer Security*, 6(3), pp. 151–180.

KPMG. (1997). 'Business organisations' fraud survey'. *KPMG Report*, Sydney, Australia.

Kroll Global Fraud Report. (2013). *Who's got something to hide? Searching for Insider Fraud.* Available: http://fraud.kroll.com/wp-content/uploads/2013/10/FraudReport_2011–2012.pdf, Accessed 08 February 2013.

Laudise, T.M. (2008). 'Ten practical things to know about 'sensitive' data collection and protection'. *The Computer and Internet Lawyer*, 25(7), pp. 26–33.

Leon, J.F. (2008). 'Top ten tips to combat cybercrime'. *The CPA Journal*, 78(5), pp. 6–19.

Lu, Y. and Ramamurthy, K. (2011). 'Understanding the link between information technology capability and organizational agility: An empirical examination'. *Management Information System Quarterly*, 35(4), pp. 931–954.

McLaren, T.S., Head, M.M., Yuan, Y. and Chan, Y.E. (2011). 'A multilevel model for measuring fit between a firm's competitive strategies and information systems capabilities'. *Management Information System Quarterly*, 35(4), pp. 909–929.

Moore, R. (2005). *Cybercrime: Investigating High-Technology Computer Crime.* Cleveland, MS: Anderson Publishing.

Newman, G.R. and McNally, M.M. (2005). *Identity Theft Literature Review.* Washington, DC: U.S. Department of Justice.

Office for National Statistics (ONS). (2014). *Report for Crime in England and Wales.* Available: http://www.ons.gov.uk/ons/rel/crime-stats/crime-statistics/period-ending-march-2014/index.html, Accessed 22 August 2014.

Raab, C.D. (2008). 'Social and political dimensions of identity'. In: S. Fischer-Hübner, P. Duquenoy, A. Zuccato and L. Martucci (Eds.), *The Future of Identity in the Information Society.* New York: Springer, pp. 3–19.

Ransbotham, S., Mitra, S. and Ramsey, J. (2012). 'Are markets for vulnerabilities effective?' *Management Information Systems Quarterly*, 36(1), pp. 43–64.

Shah, M.H., Okeke, R.I. and Ahmed, R. (2013). 'Issues of privacy and trust in E-Commerce: Exploring customers' perspectives'. *Journal of Basic and Applied Scientific Research*, 3(3), pp. 571–577.

Sommer, P. (2012). *Digital Evidence, Digital Investigations and E-Disclosure: A Guide to Forensic Readiness for Organisations, Security Advisers and Lawyers'* (3rd edn.). London: Information Assurance Advisory Council.

3 Understand Retail Operation
Towards Internal Information Theft Prevention

3.1. INTRODUCTION

This chapter looks into retail business operation by exploring the key components—people, process, and technology—which affect information processing and data security. One thing is fascinating when working with information security professionals and retail business owners in implementing strategies to prevention internal information theft. They rarely know retail business operation. Yet they pretend to understand retail operation so they can tell business owners how to do things. Security professionals cannot tell the retail companies how to run their internal information security systems if there is a lack of thorough knowledge of retail operation. The knowledge explored in this chapter equips the reader to support and advise retail businesses on how to achieve their internal information security objectives with an acceptable level of risk. It is important that you have a far broader scope of retail operation: information transaction, technology, people and process—the four pillars of information security for effective prevention of internal information theft.

By necessity, in this guide, we must focus on all four pillars. The truth is, however, that many people ignore one or more. But this book bridges these gaps in knowledge and explains the role of people in preventing internal information theft. This is done by exploring the contribution of organisational theory and the use of people-centred strategy as the basis for management roles in the prevention of internal information theft in retail business.

Case Study 3.1   A Case of UK Online Retail Industry and Internal Information Theft

The UK online retail industry is a £9.4 billion industry, accounting for approximately 5 per cent of Gross Domestic Product, with more than 10 per cent of all employment (Gambin et al., 2012). UK online retailing comprises beauty and personal care Internet retailing, consumer electronics, consumer healthcare Internet retailing, media products Internet retailing, and other Internet retailing. According to the Centre for Retail Research, 2008–2012, UK online retailing, combined with Germany and France, accounted for 71 per cent of European online sales (Nicklin et al., 2013). Thus, the experience of UK's retail sector can be taken as an important indicator of experiences of other Organisation for Economic Co-operation and Development (OECD) countries.

UK online retailing has been one of the early adopters of electronic trading operations. UK online retailing has a long tradition of Internet-based focus. The trend for the digitisation of online retail operations and their business transactions using credit/debit cards necessitates sharing of consumers' sensitive personal identifiable data. However, the Internet offers UK retailers opportunities to match this trend but not without the problems of internal information theft to contend with.

In socio-economic terms, this industry shapes the livelihood of UK consumers and affects online consumers' ability to respond to e-commerce challenges like information theft. The UK retail sector has been characterised as one of the sectors where most of the consumers are vulnerable to information theft and information security breaches with less investment on the prevention (Forrester and Seeburger, 2013; National Fraud Authority Report, 2013). Therefore, the retail sector provides a unique setting to understand issues of internal information theft prevention, which can be used as basis for designing guides to prevent information theft in other e-businesses.

3.2. PEOPLE: PLATFORM FOR INFORMATION PROCESSING IN RETAIL BUSINESS

Several years ago, the Trustworthy Computing project by Microsoft claimed that security is people, process, and technology. Some security analysts were sceptical and criticised that Microsoft was trying to shift focus from poor security loopholes (identified in their tools) to factors it may not control. This can be an unfair analysis, considering that Microsoft's recent solutions, particularly Windows 10 and Windows Server 2012, are actually quite good when it comes to security and rate high amongst other security solutions. Hence, the need to explore the importance of people (retailers as users, suppliers and customers) as the fundamental pillar that holds up other elements—information, process and technology—that make up retail operation. This analysis can be explained thus: retail business process is how people use technology to turn data into information so that they can make informed decisions in retail operations.

Information processing in retail business operation is a complex task, and in most cases nebulous because of the network of users involved—customers, retailers and suppliers. A process may provide competitive advantage to retail business only when the channel is free from hitches of information theft. Information security professionals must focus on securing critical business information, and this can be achieved by securing information processing in retail operations. Hence, attention should be given to the nature of the information processed, the owners of the information, reasons/purpose of information processing and who shares the information. These interactions in information processing create various avenues and mechanisms to use and store information. Consequently, these elements represent possible areas of weakness, as well as weak points that reduce the user's ability to visualise the process and the challenges it may pose to retail operation. The less complex or more streamlined a process, the easier to manage and secure.

In fact, inability to understand the scope of information processing in retail operation is one of the key causes of internal information theft and accidental/unintentional information leakages. As information security professionals, we must thoroughly understand the role management plays in information processing to direct retail internal information theft prevention strategies. Figure 3.1 illustrates people as the platform for information processing in retail business operation.

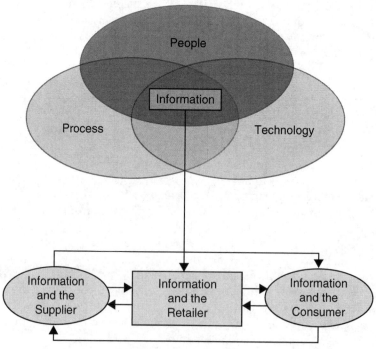

Figure 3.1   People as a Platform for Information Processing in Retail Business

Table 3.1 below summarises the processing of data in retail business. This table provides a description of forms of information that are processed in retail businesses, owners of information that are being processed, reasons/purpose for processing the information and who shares the information.

3.3. ROLE OF PEOPLE IN THE PREVENTION OF INTERNAL INFORMATION THEFT

Some internal information theft prevention guides are not designed based on people-oriented security, or, rather, integration of both technology-based software security and human contributions. In other cases, companies have depended solely on implementation of software-based security and have neglected to consider integrating people, process, and technology.

Some information prevention strategies failed due to overdependence of information security professionals on software-based security. Software-based security grounded in technology can be the most reliable in providing information availability, confidentiality and integrity, but cannot be a

Table 3.1 Information Processing in Retail Business

Forms of information	Customer/business name, date of birth, house address, job status, financial status, social circumstances, marriage status, lifestyle, visual images, race/ethnicity, health status, age, religion, etc.
Owners of information	Customers, suppliers, employers, employees, outsourcing companies, consultants, complainants, donors, lenders, clients, enquirers, victims of crimes, suspected offenders, vulnerable people, service providers, representatives, educators, trade unions, business associates, advisers, etc.
Reasons/purpose	Marketing, business promotion, advertisement, account maintenance, records keeping, sharing, business research, identify offenders, crime prevention and detection, membership records, staff records, criminal proceeding, order forms, warranty cards, customer rewards programmes, customer satisfaction survey, feedback, customer competition, etc.
Who shares the information	Suppliers, law enforcement agencies, credit reference agencies, financial companies, debt collection agencies, tracing agencies, business associates, police officers, security organisations, charity organisation, past/present/prospective employers, recruitment agencies, etc.

substitute for people-oriented security. People are indispensable, as information owners, custodians and users. These insights justify the need for integrating process and technology, with people as the central focus. Hence, it is necessary to discuss organisational role theory to explore the human role—the employees in integrating other essential elements needed for effective internal information theft prevention guides.

3.3.1 Organisational Role Theory

The concept of organisational role theory (ORT) is one of the five major models of role theory developed by Biddle (1986) to examine role development in organisations. The concept of ORT describes and provides insight into the purposive actions of individual employees, management and organisations, as they relate to the field in which they operate. The ORT concept has been applied by researchers in behavioural science, management, sociology, and psychology for modelling authority, responsibility, functions, and interactions associated with management positions.

In their study of how organisations can prevent crimes in their respective business domain, Ekblom (2010) and Sarnecki (2005) looked into the concepts of ORT and suggested that employees in business organisations should in some way complement the shared roles and responsibilities, supporting each other in the environment where they operate. Ekblom (2010) argues that it might be helpful to conceptualise people's roles in crime prevention to provide an integration platform for software-based technology, process and people, because it focuses on the 'root causes'—lack of clarity of integrated internal information prevention practices.

Biegelman (2009) agrees with Ekblom (2010) and suggests a need for interdependence of roles of the complementary management team for them to thrive in crime prevention in business organisations. Savirimuthu and Savirimuthu (2007) and Luhmann (2004) agree with these suggestions and argue that a deeper understanding of interdependence of management roles in business organisations is an important prerequisite to development of a strategic and coherent crime prevention guideline. The effective analysis of people's roles in retail operation can provide in-depth understanding of how the efforts of information security professionals could be directed toward preventing internal information theft. The interaction of security professionals and retail management becomes a role-based process in which each party begins to share the roles of the other, with a clear view of the value of effective internal information theft prevention. The interaction of various roles of human resources involved in internal information theft prevention can help to explain the management roles and the implication of their relationship with other management (IT security, data compliance, law enforcement agencies, etc.) and how it can help to minimise employee engagement in internal information theft. In addition, it can to help explain the impact of the clarity of management roles/responsibilities and how it can help to maximise management performance in providing effective internal data security.

3.3.2 People-Centred Strategy in the Prevention of Internal Information Theft

It has been understood from Chapter 1 that it is the people aspect of information processing that gets online retail organisations into most of the security loopholes. Thus, it is necessary to equip people by building their intelligence and decision-making capabilities to achieve the goal of internal information theft prevention. Retail companies can invest on physical and technical measures, such as authentication mechanisms, firewalls, and penetration and intrusion detection systems to defend against external cyberattacks. However, the insiders who have authorisation can bypass those measures to steal critical information from a business.

Insiders are familiar with internal policies, process and procedures, which could be bypassed and exploited to carry out internal information theft. Anderson et al. (2005) suggest that information theft risk management should involve a comprehensive combination of behavioural, organisational and technical issues. Since internal identity theft criminals utilise both technology and human techniques to perpetrate their threats, it is important to consider a combination of behavioural, organisational process and technical issues to prevent them. Anderson et al. (2005, p. 8), who worked on the Preliminary System Dynamics Maps of the Insider Cyber-threat Problem, reaffirmed that;

> . . . because insiders are legitimate users of their organisation's networks and systems, sophisticated technical capability is not necessarily required to carry out an insider attack. On the other hand, technically capable insiders are able, and have, carried out more sophisticated attacks, that can have more immediate, widespread impact, . . . these technical insiders also sometimes have the capability to "cover their tracks" so that identification of the perpetrator is more difficult . . .

This statement suggests that it is important to understand the basic need of employee roles in implementing retail information systems security to mitigate internal information theft risks. That is, it is important to understand the roles of the offender and users to regulate the way process and technology interacts. Since IS security management is processed by the use of procedure driven by people, the major focus of internal information theft prevention guide should be on people. Procedure, as described by ISO 9001:2000, is a way in which people—the IS security management—work to accomplish a task. The task here, as shown in Figure 3.2, is the sequence of steps and actions that are essential for prevention of internal information theft in retail businesses.

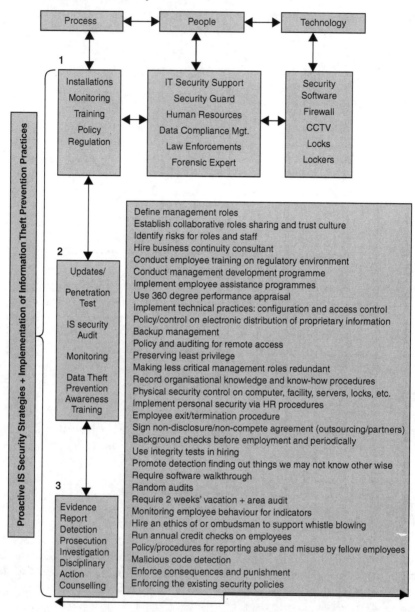

Figure 3.2   People-Centred Roles in the Prevention of Internal Information Theft

The structured tasks are designed to function as a continuous process which shows how the IS security management can implement the recommended practices to reduce internal information theft risks. The recommended practices are synthesised from the suggested internal information theft prevention practices. The practices synthesised in this section are not a comprehensive list of all the applicable information theft prevention practices. However, the practices are summarised to meet the scope of this book, which is to provide an internal information theft prevention guideline. This aim extends to clarify the task of internal information prevention and identify how the roles of management can be aligned to meet the goal of preventing information theft in retail businesses.

This task of getting people, process and technology to interact and cooperate is difficult to achieve. This is why the human vector—people—has remained the weakest link in maintaining strategic retail information systems security. This is why most internal information theft *modus operandi*—social engineering, abetted collusion and collaboration— build their attack strategies on human foibles. The human being, with lack of awareness and human desire for money or 'just wanting to help out', would always be a prime target of information theft perpetrators.

Based on the structure of Figure 3.2 above, it is important that direct relationships exist with each management role. Each of the separate boxes linked with thin arrows are indirectly related; those linked with thick arrows are directly related. The arrow links depict the level of priority given to the labelled boxes: 'box 1' and 'box 2'; if those roles, in relation to the responsibilities under the process, fail, then 'box 3' would be required. For instance, 'box 1', which is linked to 'people' with a thick arrow, comprises: IT security, data compliance, security guards and HR. It contains IS security management roles that have the possibility of sharing similar roles with each other. Figure 3.2 demonstrates the holistic interaction of both offender-oriented (people-focused) and situation-oriented (technology-focused) approaches to preventing internal information theft.

3.3.3 Management Roles in the Prevention of Internal Information Theft

This concept can improve retail information security management approaches by providing the capacity to control and monitor the technological aspects of security, as well as management adherence to established processes and procedures. In addition, it enhances the ability of IS security governance to leverage human factors by regulating their interactions with technology. It would promote intelligent workflows and process IS security management against potential internal information theft risks by aligning the skills with management roles and functions.

There are three specific constructs that explain what management does: roles, functions and skills. Although these constructs are directly or indirectly related, they can be used to analyse employees and cross management behaviour. For instance, management roles are described based on different interrelated categories: decision-making, interpersonal relationship, transfer of information, reflection, taking actions, etc.

The combination of these categories has direct influence on the responsibility of information security professional in relation to the tasks of internal information theft prevention. In implementing task of internal information theft prevention, as noted above, it is important for every security management team to have a clear role for the management to collaborate. Collaboration of management roles is vital for a comprehensive internal information theft prevention framework since the tasks and roles are the basis for the control of retail information security operations. So it is important that management roles interact and work together to support other cross-functional management. Table 3.2 below summarises the descriptions of the key management roles common in online retail companies. The interrelated steps shown in Figure 3.2 above have already described how the processes and technology can be centred on these management roles.

Table 3.2   Management Roles for Information Theft Prevention in the Retail Business

Roles	Roles description in relation to internal information prevention
Operational Management	Those that work in retail call centres and use screening techniques to process customers' order for possible abnormality or mismatch of identity attributes—name, date of birth, account detail, etc. It requires the management to ensure that personal identifiable information documents—customer and business—are cross-shredded before their disposal. For effective operation of this management, it is the role of HR to ensure that proper and essential training is provided.
Technical management	These are the software engineers, web designers and data miners that use software security tools such as authentication kits, address verification system, digital signature, and encryption. This management depends on IS/T support to protect the IS security infrastructure from potential information theft risks.
Managerial and Policy	This is the role of the management that ensures the development of explicit policy regarding protection of security and privacy of business and customers. This involves implementation of policy strategy for safe preservation of business and consumers' data. This should emphasise the ethic of the company and reinforce rewarding of employees. This would encourage and promote honesty in the workplace.
Risk Management	This role involves use of intelligent and strategic techniques to identify information theft risks such as inconsistencies in the transaction or customer's order pattern. It compares a consumer's past and present history for inconsistencies, such as case of irregularity in use of credit card within short period of time.
Resource and Control Management	This role demands the contribution of HR in counselling and training of employees. Since employees are the prime vector of information theft, there should be effective employee control. In addition, this role manages vetting and screening of employees.

3.3 SUMMARY OF CHAPTER 3

This chapter has provided knowledge of the roles management plays as people in the prevention of internal information theft. It has analysed how the role of people, as managers of information, can be considered as the basis for implementing effective internal information security while using technology for information processing in retail operations. A more technologically advanced retail company with better information processing guided by effective security management is more capable of preventing internal information theft than one without. From an information security perspective, processing information through the complex technology-oriented operations of modern retail business is problematic. But an in-depth understanding of the role of people in information processing could boost the security of retail business operation. Technology in retail business operations often adds complexity, and complexity can breed insecurity. Thus, people, process and technology must interact, and the smoothness of this interaction, in relation to security of information, is totally dependent on the role of people—the management. The management should ensure the effective security of all possible points of interaction in information-processing channels, irrespective of who owns/shares/stores the information.

However, sometimes it is impossible to provide 'effective' security for technical reasons. In such situations in retail business operations, the only way is to minimise the chances of internal information theft by adopting strategies that are applicable in retail businesses. The next discussion of this guide, Chapter 4, provides knowledge of internal information theft prevention frameworks and their practical setbacks.

REFERENCES

Anderson, D., Cappelli, D., Gonzalez, J., Mojahedzdeh, M., Moore, A. and Rich, E.(2005). 'Preliminary system dynamics maps of the insider cyber-threat problem'. Group Modelling Workshop at Software Engineering Institute, pp. 8–36.

Biddle, B.J. (1986). 'Recent developments in role theory'. *Annual Review of Sociology*, **12**, pp. 67–92.

Biegelman, M.T. (Ed.). (2009). *Identity Theft Handbook: Detection, Prevention and Security*. Hoboken, NJ: John Wiley and Sons, Inc.

Ekblom, P. (2010). *Crime Prevention, Security and Community Safety with the 5Is Framework*. Basingstoke, UK: Palgrave Macmillan.

Forrester and Seeburger. (2013). 'The future of data security and privacy: Controlling big data'. In: The WebCast, *The Silent Enemy: Preventing Data Breaches from Insiders*, 13 March 2013 at 13:00–14:00 EDT.

Gambin, L., Hogarth, T., Atfield, G., Li, Y., Breuer, Z. and Richard, G. (2012). 'Sector skills insights: Retail. UK Commission for employment and skills'. Joint Research Report, pp. 1–89.

Luhmann N. (2004). *Law as a Social System*. Oxford: Blackwell, pp. 64–66.

National Fraud Authority Report. (2013). *Annual Fraud Indicator*. London: NFA, pp. 7–32.

Nicklin, T., Meyer, K., Hardy, R. and Wilkins, N. (2013). *Cambridge Marketing Handbook: Digital—Cambridge Marketing Handbooks*. London: Kogan Page Publishers, pp. 12–15.

Sarnecki, J. (2005). *Knowledge-Based Crime Prevention, Theoretical Points of Departure for Practical Crime Prevention*. Thailand: UN Congress on Crime Prevention and Criminal Justice, pp. 1–11.

Savirimuthu, A. and Savirimuthu, J. (2007). 'Identity theft and systems theory: The Fraud Act 2006 in perspective'. Unscripted, UK.

4 Internal Information Theft Prevention Frameworks and Their Implications

1. INTRODUCTION

This chapter provides knowledge of internal information theft prevention frameworks. The empirical analysis provided here is based on the findings of reviewed information theft prevention frameworks. Some of the existing internal information theft prevention frameworks aimed to provide generic guides across business organisations. This issue of lack of a specific framework for a particular business organisation, like retail industry, justifies the need for this guide. Thus, the existing frameworks are reviewed to identify their limitations and to provide direction on how security and crime prevention managers, in retail businesses, can avoid such limitations. Cappelli et al. (2006b) advocate that the effectiveness of internal information theft prevention relies on how management adapts available frameworks and applies them in the context of their business operations.

The Cambridge Advanced Learner's Dictionary defined a framework as *a system of rules, ideas, beliefs or a supporting structure* around which something can be built that is used to plan or decide something. However, few or none of the existing frameworks focus on a *specific structure* of information theft and business sector to design the prevention for the specific requirement. The majority of available information theft frameworks are designed based on generic concepts (e.g., technology architecture and the generic nature of crimes). In some information theft prevention frameworks, the concepts of the frameworks are underpinned by research aims and objectives. Hence, as advocated by Burkhalter and Crittenden (2010), understanding of generic frameworks would enable security and crime prevention practitioners to understand and identify the research gaps needed for the recommendation of security guidelines.

4.2. GENERIC INFORMATION THEFT PREVENTION FRAMEWORKS

Several studies (e.g., Kardell, 2007; ACFE, 2014) agree that less attention has been given to the studies of internal information theft prevention in the context of a particular business organisation like online retail. Yang and Wang (2011) agree that generic internal information theft prevention frameworks might be too complex to be adapted in some business sectors because of differences in business operations, processes, organisational culture and technology. ACFE (2014) noted that there is need for security and crime prevention practitioners to understand the internal information prevention needs of a particular business sector with critical emphasis on managing the roles of security, people and processes. In his research paper, Adams (2008) also noted that although internal information theft is a common crime across business organisations, the study should be designed within a scope of policy makers in a particular business sector. Cappelli et al. (2006b) agree that the need to align business requirements with roles of management is indispensable for prevention of internal information theft.

Cappelli et al. opined that the effective synergy of efforts interplayed with IT executives, managers, technical employee, human resources, and security officers could be a practicable tool in the prevention of internal information theft. The successful implementation of the US Department of Homeland Security and Cyber Security Project confirmed the need for the deployment of effective management roles in preventing internal information theft in business sectors. In their research project, Cappelli et al. (2006a) and Moore et al. (2008) agree that since internal information theft involves primarily human elements manipulating IS, it would take the comprehensive and strategic roles of human—the management—within a defined business environment to counter the crimes. Savirimuthu and Savirimuthu (2007) suggest that a deeper understanding of the implications of managing information security in retail business is an important prerequisite to applicable information theft prevention frameworks.

Savirimuthu and Savirimuthu suggested that the integration of complementary management with IT security management would be a suitable strategy for mitigation of information theft because these crimes are motivated not only technologically but mostly socially. In agreement, Wang, Yuan and Archer (2006) acknowledge the need to provide a guide for effective development and deployment of a framework for prevention of information theft from the perspective of management roles within a defined business sector.

In addition, Lacey and Cuganesan (2005) suggested that the collaborative effort of 'human resource security'—IT management, complementary data security and crimes prevention team are often overlooked in the formulation of information theft prevention in existing frameworks. Shah and Okeke (2011) agreed with Lacey, and pointed out that available frameworks fail to prevent these crimes because the strategies do not incorporate the roles of the complementary management teams (auditing, outsourcing firms, credit monitory firms, law enforcement agency, etc.). Table 4.1 summarises the frameworks for information theft prevention.

Table 4.1 Studies on Information Theft Prevention Frameworks

Authors	Research focus	Key concepts	Research contribution
Shah and Okeke (2012)	Examination of the roles of management in information theft prevention and internal data security.	Role-based framework for analysing prevention of internal identity theft related crimes: case study in UK retail industry.	A systematic and integrated approach where key components of management work in unison is required to prevent information theft and maximise internal data security.
Steinbart et al. (2011)	Exploratory investigation of the relationship between internal audit and IS security.	An exploratory model of the factors that influence the nature of relationship between ISA and IS security functions	The proficiency of the IS security auditors affects the quality of the ISA practices and could contribute to prevention of internal information theft.
Shah and Okeke (2011)	Exploration of existing literature on the propagation of information theft, and the conceptualisation of these crimes in the retail industry.	The synthesis of role-based framework for prevention of information theft in retail industry.	Information theft prevention strategy should incorporate a collaboration of external and internal crime prevention actors, and all levels of an organisation should be given clear and specific responsibilities regarding internal data security.
Sharariri and Lababidi (2011)	Examination of the factors affecting internal auditors in the protection of computerised accounting IS from electronic penetration in banking operation	Enhancement of the factors that would contribute to the effective utilisation of ISA in protecting computerised accounting IS.	IS auditors should be fully aware of the operations of business organisations, the activities of the e-fraud prevention team to be able to proffer IS security against internal data breaches and attacks
Moorthy et al. (2011)	Evaluation of the impact of the role of IT on ISA in business organisation	Impact of the information technology on internal data security auditing.	Information Systems auditor has the responsibility of ensuring that the management and board of directors understand the liability of potential data security risks.

(*Continued*)

Table 4.1 (Continued)

Authors	Research focus	Key concepts	Research contribution
Schulze and Shah, (2009)	Investigation of communication strategies used by the e-commerce organisations (via websites) to battle identity theft related crimes.	Development of the Support—Trust—Empowerment—Prevention (STEP) method for battling identity theft related crimes.	Few e-commerce organisations proactively prevent identity theft, provide supporting actions and inform consumers on how to protect their data against such crimes.
Ji, Smith-Chao and Min (2008)	The examination of a theoretical view of identity theft crimes as the basis for business organisational information system designs (from system planner's perspective).	Systems Plan for combating identity theft—a theoretical framework.	Various roles and the relationship of the identity chain should be coordinated in designing collaborative systems for combating identity theft crimes in business
Jamieson, Winchester, Stephens and Smith (2008)	The study of formation of identity fraud profiling definition, construction of a profiling classification; and identification of the barriers to the use of profiling by business organisations.	Development of a conceptual framework for identity fraud profiling and provision of frameworks main elements, their relationships.	Organisational identity fraud based profiling methodologies have information processing techniques applicable to developing fraud profiling models in the IS in business organisations; and that integration of these techniques reduce the incidents of identity crimes.
Vasiu (2004)	Examination of the risks of e-fraud in an integrated supply chain, and overview of significant adverse effect of e-fraud as a hindrance towards achievement of business organisational IS strategic objectives.	Development of a conceptual framework for e-fraud control in integrated supply chain of business organisations.	E-fraud prevention should be integrated to incorporate board-level organisations' practices and business plans; and that management should be responsible for implementation and coordination of the human, technological, and financial resources necessary for controlling e-fraud in business organisations.
Wright (1998)	Exploration of the need for IS education among business organisations' employees	Development of a framework for IS security training for employees.	To improve IS security against information theft, IS education must be integrated into the business organisations' practices and their data protection policies.

4.3. SOFTWARE-BASED INFORMATION THEFT PREVENTION FRAMEWORKS

The British Retail Consortium (BRC) (2011) suggests that most of the existing information theft prevention frameworks (e.g., McCormick, 2008; Jabbour and Menasce, 2009) have focused on the implementation of software security. Others researchers (e.g., Bishop and Gates, 2008; Niekerk and Solms, 2010) focus on the combination of technology and process, while a few (e.g., Collins, 2003; Moore et al., 2008) attempt to combine technology, process and people. The resulting frameworks from software-based studies are the scientific approaches that are only implementable in computer systems (Jamieson et al., 2009).

For instance, Le Lievre and Jamieson's (2005) preconception of a model of identity fraud profiling was built based on information processing, which uses the trails from the computer systems to analyse the behaviour of the perpetrators. This framework application relies more on the use of computer systems than on the contribution of the IS management roles and end-users. This neglect of the contribution of these roles is one of the major challenges that security and crime prevention practitioners would need to tackle to achieve effective information theft prevention.

An analysis of the literature shows that many studies have neglected a crucial element of people: management roles. From Table 4.2 below, software-based frameworks built with the concept of technology dominated information theft prevention studies. 10 out of the 16 identified information theft prevention models were designed and deployed based on technology.

For instance, Nelliker (2010) and Park and Giordano (2006) applied the role-based access control techniques for analyses of information theft criminals' behaviours and profiles.

While Jabbour and Menasce (2009) present the Insider Threat Security Architecture (ITSA) framework to analyse the case of IS security compromised by privileged user, Ha et al. (2007) applied a capability acquisition graph to demonstrate criminal threats. These techniques are implementable only on computer systems. The two models that are based on the concepts of the process by Niekerk and Solms (2010) and Bishop and Gates (2008) present a conceptual model that contributes to the argumentation of the organisational culture in information security systems. Only the system dynamics model and the MERIT model by Moore et al. (2008) and Greitzer et al. (2008), Cappelli et al. (2006b) with Keeney et al. (2005) integrated these key elements: people, process and technology to design and deploy an information theft prevention framework.

While it is theoretically possible for these contributions to IS systems security practices to reduce internal data security vulnerabilities and bolster internal information theft prevention, researchers (e.g., Hofmeyr et al., 1998; Allen et al., 1999) suggest that it is practically infeasible unless the roles of human are central to information theft prevention strategies and practices.

Table 4.2 Information Theft Prevention Frameworks Based on Technology, Process and People

Prevention Concepts	Researchers	Focus of the Model	Number of Studies
Process	Niekerk and Solms (2010)	Conceptual model	2
	Bishop and Gates (2008)	Analyses of the information theft threats	
Technology	Nellikar (2010)	Scalable Simulation Framework	10
	Jabbour and Menasce (2009)	Insider Threat Security Architecture	
	McCormick (2008)	EDLP Programme	
	Ha et al. (2007)	ICMAP	
	Park and Giordan (2006)	Role-based Access Control	
	Butts (2006)	SPM-IT / MAMIT approach	
	Chinchani, Iyer, Ngo and Upadhyaya (2005)	End user security behaviours	
	Symonenko et al. (2004)	Natural Language Processing Systems (NLPS)	
	Schultz (2002)	6 indicator framework	
	Anderson et al. (2000)	8 general approaches	
People, Process and Technology	Moore et al. (2008); Band et al. (2006)	System dynamics	4
	Greitzer et al. (2008); Cappelli et al. (2006b); Keeney et al. (2005)	MERIT	

4.4. WHY DO THE FRAMEWORKS FAIL IN PREVENTING INFORMATION THEFT?

The information theft prevention frameworks that have been discussed above cover some essential suggestions for the application and integration of process and software security. However, these suggestions have not yielded effective outcomes in relation to the huge IT security investment made by most retail companies. For instance, PriceWaterCoopers (PWC)

(2014) suggests that even though more than 50 per cent of companies in the UK have adopted most practices recommended in these frameworks and plan to spend more on IT security, 67 per cent of the companies expect a rise in information theft incidents.

It is vital to ask why these prevention practices and frameworks discussed above arguably do not contribute to effective prevention of information theft incidents. Vaca (2003) argues that some online retail companies that seem to comply with the prevention practices do have the capacity to provide effective and efficient strategies that ensure quality requirements and cost reduction. Other studies (e.g., Popa and Doinea, 2007; Dean et al., 2012; Forrester and Seeburger, 2013; PriceWaterCoopers (PWC), 2014) agrees that many online retail companies attributed their failure to the lack of resources, or that their company is apparently not big enough to accommodate an IS security departments and maintenance routine costs. In addition to these reasons, the majority of the businesses cannot answer fundamental IS security issue questions related to;

- Performance measurement (how well is the IS security enhancing business requirement?)
- Security control profiling (what IS security processes are important, and what are the critical success factors for control?)
- IS security awareness (what are the risks of not achieving the internal data security objectives?)
- Benchmarking (what do other businesses do, and how can their results be compared and measured?).

In addition to answering these questions, from insights provided from the literature, most of the frameworks and practices for prevention of internal information theft failed because of the following reasons:

- The perception that adequate and advanced IS security tools are already in place;
- Fragmented roles within the IS security management team;
- Security and crime prevention management negligence;
- The huge demand on companies to maintain the increasing PID/I used by the consumers via e-tailing and e-commerce;
- The cost of Information System/Technology (IS/T) security management;
- The perception of low expectations from the IS security and compliance management by the business managers.

The perception that adequate and advanced IS security tools are already in place: Company managers sometimes believe that having security software and firewalls, and being Sarbenes-Oxley (SOX), PCI and ISO related compliant are enough. They fail to know that, unless these controls and regulations are consistently checked, the effectiveness of their security might not be assured. Dean et al. (2012) suggests that it took more than 5,000 companies until 2008 to join the International Association of Data Privacy that was founded in 2000. PriceWaterCoopers (PWC) (2014) indicated that 80 per cent of companies fail to evaluate their spending on IS security resources or review if they are properly implemented and regulated. PWC (2014) suggests that most companies struggle to evaluate their data security tools and regulations only in the aftermath of information theft incidents. Bielski (2005) agrees with this suggestion that few companies make strategic investments in their IT security.

Non-alignment of roles between the IS security management team: Shah and Okeke (2011) noted that some businesses lack integrated data security approaches between the external and internal security auditors. In some cases, there is segregation in the roles of the sourcing and outsourcing security companies between the business and law enforcement agencies. For an effective proactive measure in the prevention of internal information theft, they suggested that the business IS management and the security audit team have to work in unison and jettison the perception of role segregation between cross-functional management.

Management negligence: The evolving information theft risks and threats that might demand new tools and procedures are often treated with laxity by business owners, security and crime prevention management. At times, some of the security tools and regulations are not applied effectively. In PriceWaterCoopers' survey (PWC) (2014), 56 per cent of businesses did not carry out any security checks of their external providers; instead they only relied on contracts and contingency plans. IS security-resource implementations can be effective only if they are well reviewed, regulated and properly applied. Many companies have fallen into this bandwagon of aftermath effect of internal information theft. PriceWaterCoopers' (PWC) (2014) tracking of the past three years shows the degrading capabilities of IS security management across business organisations. In 2011, only 41 per cent of approximately 10, 000 executives across business organisations in 138 countries acknowledged that they have data security compliance and identity management strategy, compared to 48 per cent in 2009. While only 39 per cent of these executives acknowledged that they reviewed their data security policies and regulations annually in 2011, more than 52 per cent did in 2009. With an increasing reliance of the companies on software security, the majority of companies depend on contingency plans to rectify security flaws after incidents of information theft are perpetrated by criminals.

The huge demand on companies to maintain the increasing PID/I used by the consumers via e-tailing and e-commerce: An average retail company today handles at least five million customers' PID/I, which encourages decentralisation of the data storage. This practice leads to vulnerabilities related to file transfer protocols (FTP), network shares and e-mail, which in turn pose many challenges, including large file management, FTP software process, audit trails and version control, etc. (Forrester and Seeburger, 2013).

The cost of Information System/Technology (IS/T) security management: The ACFE (2014) survey suggests that some of the companies apparently consider themselves too small to bear the cost of applying security auditing for information theft prevention. The failure of the business executives to conduct a cost and benefit analysis of IS security investments often leads them to believe that security costs outweigh the benefits. PriceWaterCoopers' (PWC) (2014) survey indicated that 12 per cent of senior management give less priority to data compliance management.

The perception of low expectations from the IS security and compliance management by the business managers: Popa and Doinea (2007) noted that many businesses managers often do not trust the capabilities of their security audit and compliance management. In some cases, companies perceive data security audits as a complex practice and become intimidated by the daunting and demanding tasks of data security management. In some cases, vulnerability and penetration tests are perceived by the business owners as a hindrance that may affect the effective running of business operations. Business owners tend to put business gains ahead of the security risks associated with information theft. In summary, there are some factors identified in the research review which can contribute to poor implementation of information theft prevention frameworks. They include:

- Poor understanding of the nature of internal information theft by IS security and crime prevention management (Newman and McNally, 2005; Schreft, 2007);
- Absence of comprehensive frameworks, strategy and data security tools (Abagnale, 2007; Jakobsson and Myers, 2007); if they exist, these frameworks for prevention were developed in the context of generic business organisations which might be inapplicable to particular businesses such as retail industry (CIFAS[1], 2010; BRC, 2011);
- Overdependence on software security, which may lead to inadequate monitoring of privileged users of information systems (Mills, 2007; Acoca, 2008).
- Lack of understanding of the role of people in integrating people, process and technology (Keeney et al., 2005; Cappelli et al., 2006b; Moore et al., 2008).

4.5. SUMMARY OF CHAPTER 4

This chapter has explored the available information theft prevention frameworks and their practical implementation issues. The failure of most of the frameworks can be attributed to the lack of clear roles and responsibilities given to security managers and administrators, which in turn might lead to other related issues summarised in Case Study 4.2. These issues provide background on comprehensive internal information theft prevention practices and knowledge that could be extended in designing effective security strategies by retail management. In addition, the knowledge provides insight into the imperative for evaluative research to assess how the requirements of the frameworks are met for successful implementation of subsequent prevention practices in online retail companies. The challenges of effectively implementing the frameworks have been, in some cases, cited as the reason that some internal information prevention practices have failed. However, the failure of the practices have left management with little or no better option than to resort to the available coercive security strategies (software security). But with this option, yet another question is whether the choice leaves us better off. If yes, the unavoidable question still remains: why have the software-based frameworks, like the ones identified in this chapter, failed? Chapter 4 provides answers to this question by identifying organisational challenges that are being faced by information security management in preventing internal information theft in retail businesses.

REFERENCES

Abagnale, F.W. (2007). *Stealing Your Life: The Ultimate Identity Theft Prevention Plan*. New York: BroadwayBooks, The Crown Publishing Group.

Acoca, B. (2008). 'Online identity theft'. *Organisation of Economic Cooperation and Development (OECD) Observer*, **268**, pp. 12–13.

Adams, C. (2008). 'No certainty yet for identity assurance: The need for assuring identity is clear, but the path to achieving it is no'. *Signal*, **63**(1), pp. 83–86.

Allen, J., Christie, A., Fithen, W., McHugh, J., Pickel, J. and Stoner, E (1999). 'State of the practice of intrusion detection technologies'. Tech. Rep. CMU/SEI-99-TR-028, Carnegie Mellon University/Software Engineering Institute, pp. 1–111.

Anderson, R.H., Bozek, T., Longstaff, T., Meitzler, W., Skroch, M. and Wyk, K.V. (2000). 'Research on mitigating the insider threat to information systems'. Proceedings of a Workshop Held in RAND Corporation, Santa Monica, pp. 1–35.

Association of Certified Fraud Examiners (ACFE). (2014). 'Report to the nations on occupational fraud and abuse: Global fraud study'. Available: http://www.acfe.com/rttn/docs/2014-report-to-nations.pdf, Accessed 20 April 2014.

Band, S.R., Cappelli, D.M., Fischer, L.F., Moore, A.P., Shaw, E.D. and Trzeciak, R.F. (2006). 'Comparing insider IT sabotage and espionage: A model based analysis'. CMU/SEI-2006-TR-026.

Bielski, L. (2005). 'Will you spend to thwart ID theft?' *ABA Banking Journal*, **97**(4), pp. 54–62.

Bishop, M. and Gates, C. (2008). 'Defining the insider threat', Proceedings of the 4th annual workshop on Cyber security and information intelligence research: Developing strategies to meet the cyber security and information intelligence challenges ahead.

British Retail Consortium (BRC). (2011). *Retail Crime and Loss Prevention Report*. Available: http://www.brc.org.uk/brc_news_detail.asp?id=2065, Accessed 12 February 2012.

e755 e ment>

Burkhalter, C. and Crittenden, J. (2010). 'Professional identity theft: What is it? Are we contributing to it?' What can we do to stop it?' *Contemporary Issues in Communication Science and Disorders*, 35, pp. 89–94.

Butts, J.W. (2006). 'Formal mitigation strategies for the insider threat: A security model and risk analysis framework'. Available: https://www.afresearch.org/skins/rims/q_mod_be0e99f3-fc56–4ccb-8dfe 670c0822a153/q_act_downloadpaper/q_obj_9390d5ea-5e71–4abb-b3e6-c03c79975762/display.aspx, Accessed 9 October 2012.

Cappelli, D.M., Desai, A.G., Moore, A.P., Shimeall, T.J., Weaver, E.A. and Willke, B.J. (2006a). 'Management and education of the risk of insider threat (MERIT): Mitigating the risk of sabotage to employers' information, systems, or networks.' Proceedings of the 24th International System Dynamics Conference, Nijmegen, Netherlands, July.

Cappelli, D.M., Desai, A.G., Moore, A.P., Shimeall, T.J., Weaver, E.A. and Willke, B.J. (2006b). 'System dynamics modeling of computer system sabotage'. Joint CERT Coordination Center/SEI and CyLab at Carnegie Mellon University Report, Pittsburgh, PA, pp. 1–34.

Chinchani, R., Iyer, A., Ngo, H.Q. and Upadhyaya, S. (2005). 'Towards a theory of insider threat, assessment'. Proceedings of the 2005 International Conference on Dependable Systems and Networks, Yokohama, Japan, pp. 108–117.

CIFAS: The UK's Fraud Prevention Service, (2010). 'Staff Fraudscape: Depicting the UK's staff fraud landscape', Available: http://www.cifas.org.uk/secure/content PORT/uploads/documentsCIFAS%20Reports/CIFAS_Staff_Fraudscape_May_2010.pdf, Accessed 29 November 2011.

Collins, J.M. (2003). 'National Institute of Justice Crime Report'. U.S. Department of Justice, Office of Justice Programs, Michigan State University, USA.

Dean, S., Pett, J., Holcomb, C., Roath, D. and Sharma, N. (2012). 'Fortifying your defences: The role of internal audit in assuring data security and privacy'. PCW Publications. Available: http://www.PWC.com/us/en/risk-assurance-services/publications/internal-audit-assuring-data-security-privacy.jhtml, Accessed 9 October 2012.

Forrester and Seeburger. (2013). 'The future of data security and privacy: Controlling big data'. In: The WebCast, *The Silent Enemy: Preventing Data Breaches from Insiders*, 13 March 2013 at 13:00–14:00 EDT.

Greitzer, F.L., Moore, A.P., Cappelli, D.M., Andrews, D.H., Carroll, L.A. and Hull, T.D. (2008). 'Combating the insider cyber threat'. *IEEE Security and Privacy*, 6(1), pp. 61–64.

Ha, D., Upadhayaya, S., Ngo, H., Pramanik, S., Chinchani, R. and Mathew, S. (2007). 'Insider threat analysis using information-centric modelling'. *International Federation for Information Processing*, 242(2007), pp. 55–73.

Hofmeyr, S.A., Forrest, S. and Somayaji, A. (1998). 'Intrusion detection using sequences of systems calls'. *Journal of Computer Security*, 6(3), pp. 151–180.

Jabbour, G. and Menasce, D.A. (2009). 'The insider threat security architecture: A framework for an integrated, inseparable, and uninterrupted self-protection mechanism'. International Conference on Computational Science and Engineering, CSE '09, pp. 1616–1620.

Jakobsson, M. and Myers, S. (2007). *Phishing and Countermeasures: Understanding the Increasing Problems of Electronic Identity Theft*. Hoboken, NJ: John Wiley and Sons.

Jamieson, R J., Winchester, D W., Stephens, G. and Smith, S. (2008). 'Developing a conceptual framework for identity fraud profiling'. Proceedings of the 16th European Conference on Information Systems at the J.E. Cairnes Graduate School of Business and Public Policy, National University of Ireland, Galway, Ireland, 9–11 June.

Jamieson, R., Land, L. P, W., Smith, S., Stephens, G. and Winchester, D. (2009). 'Information security in an identity management lifecycle: Mitigating identity crimes'. *AMCIS 2009 Proceedings*, pp. 1–9.

Ji, S., Smith-Chao, S. and Min, Q. (2008). 'Systems plan for combating identity theft—A theoretical framework'. *Journal of Service Science and Management*, 2008(1), pp. 143–152.

Kardell, R.L. (2007). 'Three steps to fraud prevention in the workplace'. ACFE Report to the Nation of Occupational Fraud and Abuse, pp. 16–19.

Keeney, M.M., Conway, T., Kowalski, E., Williams, M., Cappelli, D., Moore, P.M., Rogers, S. and Shimeal, T.J. (2005). 'Insider threat study: Computer system sabotage in critical infrastructure sectors'. Joint SEI and U.S. Secret Service Report, Pittsburgh, PA, pp. 1–45.

Lacey, D. and Cuganesan, S. (2005). 'The role of organisations in identity theft response: The organization–individual victim dynamic'. *Journal of Consumer Affairs*, 38(2), pp. 244–261.

Le Lievre, E., and Jamieson, R. (2005). 'An Investigation of Identity Fraud in Australian Organisations'. Collaborative Electronic Commerce Technology and Research (CollECTeR), pp. 1–10.

McCormick, M. (2008). 'Data theft: A prototypical insider threat'. *Advances in Information Security*, 39(2008), pp. 53–68.

Mills, G. (2007). *Identity Theft: Everything You Need to Know to Protect Yourself*. Sussex, UK: Summersdale Publishers.

Moore, A.P., Cappelli, D.M., Greitzer, F.L, Carroll, L.A. and Hull, T.D. Andrews, D.H. (2008). 'Combating the insider cyber threat'. *IEEE Security and Privacy*, 6(1), pp. 61–64.

Moorthy, M. K., Seetharaman, A., Zulkifflee, M., Meyyappan, G., and Lee, H. S. (2011). 'The impact of information technology on internal auditing'. *African Journal of Business Management*, 5(9), pp. 3523–3539.

Nellikar, S. (2010). 'Insider threat simulation and performance analysis of insider detection algorithms with role based model'. Electronic Master of Science Thesis, Electrical and Computer Engineering, Graduate College of the University of Illinois at Urbana-Champaign, USA, pp. 1–6. Available: https://www.ideals.illinois.edu/bitstream/handle/2142/16177/Nellikar_Suraj.pdf?sequence=2, Accessed 23 May 2011.

Newman, G.R. and McNally, M.M. (2005). *Identity Theft Literature Review*. Washington, DC: US Department of Justice.

Niekerk, R. and Solms, R.V. (2010). 'Information security culture: A management perspective'. *Computers and Security*, 29(4), pp. 476–486.

Park, J.S. and Giordano, J. (2006). 'Role-based profile analysis for scalable and accurate insider-anomaly detection'. Proceedings of the 25th IEEE International Performance Computing and Communications Conference, Workshop on Information Assurance, Phoenix, AZ, pp. 463–469.

Popa, M. and Doinea, M. (2007). 'Audit characteristics for information systems'. *Revista Informatica Economic* , 4(44), pp. 103–106.

PriceWaterCoopers (PWC). (2014). *Information Security Breach Survey (ISBS) Technical Report*. Available: https://www.gov.uk/government/uploads/system/uploads/attachment_data/file/307296/bis-14-767-information-security-breaches-survey-2014-technical-report-revision1.pdf, Accessed 02 April 2014.

Savirimuthu, A. and Savirimuthu, J. (2007). 'Identity theft and systems theory: The Fraud Act 2006 in perspective'. Unscripted, UK.

Schreft, S.L. (2007). 'Risks of identity theft: Can the market protect the payment system?'. *Economic Review—Federal Reserve Bank of Kansas City*, 92(4), pp. 5–40.

Schultz, E.E. (2002). 'A framework for understanding and predicting insider attacks'. *Computers and Security*, 21, pp. 526–531.

Schulze, M. and Shah, M.H. (2009). 'The step method battling identity theft using e-retailers' website'. Paper accepted at 9th IFIP Conference on e-Business, e-Services, and e-Society, I 3 E, Nancy, France.

Shah, H.M. and Okeke, R.I. (2011). 'A framework for internal identity theft prevention in retail industry'. Intelligence and Security Informatics Conference (EISIC), European, Athens, Greece.

Shah, M.H. and Okeke, R.I. (2012). 'Role-based framework as a model for analysing prevention of internal identity theft related crimes'. Submitted to Information and Management for review.

Sharariri, J.A. and Lababidi, M.H. (2011). 'Factors affecting the role of internal auditor in the protection of computerised accounting Information Systems from electronic penetration (A Field Study on Banks Operating in Jordan)'. *International Research Journal of Finance and Economics*, 68, pp. 140–160.

Steinbart, P.J, Raschke, R.L., Gal, G. and Dilla, W.N. (2011). 'The relationship between internal audit and information security: An exploratory investigation'. University of Waterloo Centre for Information Integrity & Information Systems Assurance 7th Biennial Research Symposium, October 20–22, 2011, pp. 1–32.

Symonenko, S., Liddy, E.D., Yilmazel, O., Zoppo, R.D. and Brown, E. (2004). 'Semantic analysis for monitoring insider threats'. IEEE International Conference on Intelligence and Security Information. Available: http://surface.syr.edu/cgi/viewcontent.cgi?article=1047&context=istpub.

Vacca, J. R. (2003). *Identity Theft*. USA: Prentice Hall PTR.

Vasiu, L. (2004). 'A conceptual framework of eFraud control in an integrated supply chain'. Proceedings of European Conference on Information Systems (ECIS), Paper 161.

Walker, A., Flatley, J., Kershaw, C and Moon, D. (2008, 09). Crime in England and Wales: Findings from the British Crime Survey and police recorded crime, Home Office Statistical Bulletin Volume 1, pp. 85–87.

Wang, W., Yuan, Y. and Archer, N. (2006). *A Contextual Framework for Combating Identity Theft, IEEE Security and Privacy*. Published by IEEE Computer Society.

Wright, M.A. (1998). 'The need for information security education'. *Computer Fraud and Security*, 1998(8), pp. 14–17.

Yang, S. and Wang, Y. (2011). 'System dynamics based insider threats modelling'. *International Journal of Network Security and Its Applications*, 3(3), pp. 1–12.

5 Challenges in Preventing Internal Information Theft

5.1 INTRODUCTION

This chapter provides reflective knowledge for security management and contributes insights on tightening the data security processes in meeting Payment Card Industry Data Security Standard (PCI DSS) requirements. Internal information thefts have been on the rise in the last few years. The most pressing challenge, among others, is the number of dishonest employees who are indulging in internal information theft-related crimes, generally because the company board and heads of security and crime prevention are not prepared to make strategic decisions on reviewing data security frameworks in the face of tightening operation budgets. The existing data security frameworks that are designed based on the PCI DSS rules for preventing information theft were not receiving sufficient financial support. However, security managers feel that their practices have improved over time and that their employers are learning from their challenges and mistakes, and they have generally tightened up their commitment on due diligence and quality data security assurance. This can be observed in terms of how security managers monitor employees and implement data security strategies while adapting to organisational challenges.

5.2. ADOPTION OF PCI DSS IN THE PREVENTION OF INTERNAL INFORMATION THEFT

PCI DSS is the main standard and requirements set out for storing payment card data. PCI DSS specifies steps which should be taken to ensure payment card data is kept safe both during and after transactions. The current PCI DSS that guides internal information theft prevention frameworks is not as prescriptive and presented as it should be for every retail business.

The PCI DSS guidelines leave it up to an individual payment card company to design its own approaches, but it does address key issues, such as, for example, the implementation of a company's internal and external data security run processes. It provides binding best practices on the need to contractually secure compliance by, and an acknowledgement of responsibility from, third-party providers. The PCI DSS framework does not spell out the ways in which data compliance managements can and can't be involved in delivery and the issue of related-party transactions as clearly as it might, and that this created internal security risk. For instance, some security experts have argued that *the issue of full implementation of PCI DSS leaves UK retailers "in a bit of a quandary" in relation to compliance with the Data Protection Act (DPA)*. This supports the Information Commissioner's Office's (ICO) suggestion in 2011 that *UK retailers that fail to store payment data in accordance with PCI DSS "or provide equivalent protection when processing customers' credit card details" could be held to be in breach of the DPA and subject to fines.*

The view that existing security checks and controls are too broad for a retail system was common across security and crime prevention managers, mostly those managements from big retail companies' perspectives. A common view is that the data compliance and security managements of big retail companies now have many more partner companies to oversee. For instance, in the case of UK retail, neither the PCI DSS nor any of the existing legislation covering personal data protection (e.g., Data Protection Act (DPA) 1998, Computer Misuse Act 1990, Privacy and Electronic Communications (EC Directive) Regulations 2003) is fit for the purpose of guarding against internal information theft. PCI DSS's interest in retail is mainly contractually secure compliance to ensure payment card data is kept safe both during and after transactions. But neither it nor the security auditing firms that undertake external security audits have the capacity and skills to get below the surface to understand the relationships that are key to understanding prevention of internal information theft (will they get below the skin?).

At best, an auditor might detect data security loopholes after the internal information theft incident when the aim should be to have preventative systems: this relies too much on managements 'within' the retail companies at present.

The PCI DSS provides guidelines for looking at data compliance snapshots but not guidelines for security auditors. As a result, there is the potential for the scale of internal information theft cases to go unnoticed for years, as seen in the reported cases above in the Chapter 2. The fact that neither the PCI DSS nor data protection legislation is really reducing cases of internal information theft is a general challenge that the security and crime prevention management working within retail companies has to deal with.

The modus operandi of the internal information theft perpetrators seems to change day to day, so there is a sense that PCI DSS should include guides for making it up as it goes along. For instance, the PCI DSS version 3 rules that were released in August 2013 by the Payment Card Industry Security Standards Council (PCI SSC) outlined a broad timetable for when UK retailers will have to comply with the new rules. However, the majority of security and crime prevention managers seem to lead, with the PCI DSS following; managers are telling them things, including about internal information theft.

Very many security heads are spending so much time playing with software technology and experimenting with internal information theft-related crime data in different formats; they invest solely in security auditors, neglecting the roles of other functional managements and becoming distracted by software solutions and/or auditors and taking their eyes off the ball.

5.3. OVERREGULATED AND DISJOINTED INFORMATION SECURITY POLICIES

Retail companies are already heavily regulated and scrutinised regarding information security policies for prevention of internal information theft. This oversight comes from a variety of sources: the IT security department, company data protection policy, employees' Code of Conduct handbook, HR and internal and external auditors. The majority of existing policies and frameworks set clear rules which every employee (managers, shop-floor staff, consultants, contractors, etc.) should adhere to when accessing and dealing with companies' personal identifiable information. The issue with various security policies is that retail companies tend to find the policies disjointed and difficult to harmonise as the companies grow. The more established retail companies work hard to tighten up their retail operation processes as they go along, generally, after a rapidly expansion; such companies would begin to struggle to cope with the demands of data compliance and regulations, which means that their security policy would not be as robust as it was early on.

Data compliance managers of large retail chains could find these issues more challenging because some of the policies may not have been clearly defined regarding security controls or operating processes. Consequently, some online retail transactions via cards are being carried out without agreed procedures for security controls. In other cases, where a large amount of operation services are outsourced to consultants and other security operating companies, these operational developments can make companies vulnerable to perpetrators of internal information theft. However, the current framework adopted by many retail companies is to assign security auditors to the outsourcing security companies run by partner small retail companies, following the decision to audit and monitor their retail operations. But with the financial capacity of some of the outsourced companies, and small size of their businesses, their level of IT security infrastructure and security capability are likely to be weak.

Even when the security auditor combines the functions of both external and internal security auditors, the auditor may be effective in the role of external security auditor and providing 'strict' PCI DSS rules but not effective at the regulatory function within the auditee (outsourced companies). This is not because of lack of resources but because the auditee won't provide the security auditor with comprehensive access. Consequently, security auditors may know the extent of the security capability and can't be confident to document the audit report. As a result, both the audit and auditee companies would be in a dilemma of either withdrawing their business contractual agreement or harmonising the security policy to provide an effective security audit.

5.4. CULTURAL ORIENTATION OF THE SECURITY AND CRIME PREVENTION MANAGEMENT

The cultural orientation of management is one of the major challenges of preventing internal information theft in retail companies. Tsai (2001) explains that cultural orientation is the degree to which employees are inclined to be actively engaged in the norms, practices and traditions of a specific organisational culture. Cameron and Quinn (1999) throw more light on the issues of culture within the organisation by defining organisational culture as a set of shared assumptions, beliefs, practices and values that direct and shape members' behaviour and attitudes. Based on these definitions, the cultural orientation of management can be the root of other challenging issues which include: management believes that IS security is a complex issues; perception that it is difficult for companies to provide an adequate budget for IT security, internal security policies and strategies and perceived information theft incidents.

5.4.1. Complexity of Information Security

The security and crime prevention managers are inclined to treat information security regarding prevention of internal information theft as a complex organisational issue often dependent on software security. Consequently, management often resists innovative policies that might be strategic in preventing information theft-related crimes. This belief reflects the reason for Chia et al.'s (2003) argument that, without change in the cultural orientation of IS security managers, the enforcement of new policies regarding computer-related crime prevention might not be optimal.

In the same vein, the cultural orientation of the management influences retail companies' decision to provide an adequate budget for IT security. For example, some boards of directors are inclined to treat budgets related to IT security as a financial burden to their company and are often reluctant to support information theft prevention initiatives. Instead of investing to improve their theft prevention strategies, the management relies on their managerial experience and contingency plans. This is evidenced by the analyses of the case studies that have been discussed in Chapter 2.

Crime prevention managers would be confident that they have got documented reports of all the procedures taken during the investigation; and that internal information theft happens over and over again. Managers often believe that handling criminal cases related to internal information theft provides them with enough practical experiences to help them in subsequent incidents; while professional analyses of information theft case files could cost a lot of money, take lots of times and expertise and require the hiring of professionals to do the analyses. Most of the internal information theft preventions may have failed in retail companies because of the management orientation that there is no need to invest in innovative IT security initiatives if there is no apparent security threat.

Some business organisations neglect strategic IS security practices because they have not had any major loss to computer crimes related threats. This suggestion supports the findings by PWC (2014) that more than 56 per cent of businesses did not carry out effective information security checks; instead they only relied on contingency plans.

In the same vein, PWC (2014) further added that retail companies apparently consider themselves '*not rich enough*' to bear the cost of IS security, while other sectors often argue that the cost of IT security investment outweighs the benefits. However, some top managers point out the reason for not investing in security tools recommended by IT security managers. The reason of not investing is because the IT security managers cannot provide clear information on the substantial impact of existing IT security that have been invested in preventing internal information theft. Their argument is that IT security management is supposed to report/publish the impact of their security strategies in preventing information theft, but when this reporting is not done it is hard to evaluate the benefits of IS security investment and strategies.

In addition, the cultural orientation of the security management can weaken the security strategies in preventing internal information theft by limiting the scope of a company's internal data security strategies and policies. In other words, the implementation of the security policies is motivated by the internal company's requirement but not based on needs and the importance of security practices. That means that security and crime prevention management considers innovative information security strategies as worth it if they fit into the policy stipulation of their company. Maynard and Ruighaver (2006) suggest that, in most cases, due to the organisational security culture, a number of business organisations are forced to conform to existing internal information compliance and security policy not because the policy is worthwhile but because it fits into their orientation.

5.4.2. Narrowly Defined Security Roles

Similarly, the issue of cultural orientation has some impacts on the responsibilities of security managers in relation to their peculiar job roles. For instance, in the case when the security managers are explicitly empowered to intervene and make independent decisions in order to address poorly designed data security tools and policies, this can be used against them if the decisions are not statutorily meant to be within the their defined job responsibility. Software engineers always continue with their major job roles, which is basically designing retail company system applications, but they neglect the need to contribute to improving internal information security—which the software engineer would argue is a role that should be left to the security and top managers to handle.

This is the case in some retail companies, where managers have to stick to their job roles with little or no contribution to the collaborative effort regarding internal data security and internal information theft prevention. Top security and crime management are saddled with roles of designing and implementing security strategies in preventing information theft-related crimes, while the shop-floor employees see internal data security regulations prevention as the business of the top management alone. However, Popa and Doinea (2007) argue that the perceived cultural orientation where only the top managers are concerned with issues of internal information theft prevention might be linked to the reason that internal information theft is a sensitive security issue as well as the complex nature of these crimes. This reason can be considerable, as some businesses managers often do not trust the capabilities of shop-floor employees because complex security practices require the expertise of top data security management. In a similar suggestion, Koh et al. (2005) added that, because of the nature of IS security, only a fraction of management is involved in implementing security strategies, and this could pose a major challenge in business organisations.

5.4.3. Classification of Information Theft Incidents

Some security management personnel believe that the amount of attention that would be given to a particular information theft incident would depend on *the nature* and *the class* of the incidents. This issue of incidents' *characteristics* and *classification* was discussed in Chapter 2 as it has influence on the amount of effort the law enforcement agency/police put into information theft investigations. In the same vein, security management believes that some incidents should be treated with respect to the characteristics of an internal information theft incident profile—*who* the perpetrator is, *where the perpetrator comes from* and what is the perpetrator's *ethnic origin*. The IS security management is inclined to think that some employees with some cultural features are more prone to perpetrating internal information theft than others.

Because of cultural influence in the way the IS security management investigates information theft incidents, some of the incidents are not given due attention because the suspect is from a developed country or belongs to an ethnic majorities. Some members of crime investigation teams would argue that most internal information theft-related crimes they have investigated are perpetrated by employees from minority ethnic groups, although sometimes there are bad ones from developed countries, but the cases from developed countries are not that bad compared to those from those minorities.

The crime prevention managers seemed to believe that employees from 'developing' or 'less developed' countries are more likely to perpetrate crimes than those from developed countries. Drawing upon this insight, that security and crime prevention management holds a biased view of law-abiding employees from minority ethnic background, Westley (1970) has explained that security officers (within the occupational roles of control) often experience hostility in the environment of ethnic minority as they perceive such environment to be prone to crimes.

In a similar study, Skolnick (1966) explains that security officers respond to crime incidents in a way that predicts the situations and perpetrators which present the greatest risk to security management. Skolnick (1966) suggests that security officers refer to such perpetrators as the *'symbolic assailant'*, which means a profile of an individual whose appearance, ethnic background and demeanour represents an indicator of criminal behaviour, irrespective of whether the individual actually commits crimes. Having this occupational culture, Cosgrove (2011) argues that security officers are inclined to be suspicious in identifying abnormal crime-related activities. In doing so, security officers gather information on innocent individuals which officers may have assumed to be at the risk of offending in a way that satisfies the perception of the symbolic assailant.

Other earlier studies (e.g., Westley, 1970; Cain, 1973; Waddington, 1999; Scerra, 2011) refer to this perception as a culture of 'racial and ethnic minorities prejudice' which is common not only in the police occupation but also in other related crime prevention settings.

5.5. STEREOTYPED ATTITUDES OF SECURITY AND CRIME PREVENTION MANAGEMENT

In particular, Scerra (2011) characterises the cultural orientation of crime prevention managers as 'investigating stereotypes', where the crime prevention managers use stereotypes in dealing with their roles, functions and practices. This issue has also been noted by Sanders and Young (2003), who point out that the cultural orientation of police work in the UK affects the way police label suspects based on their race and subsequent group. The suspects who fall within marginalised groups in society are often vulnerable to prosecution even when they are not guilty (Engel et al., 2002). However, this book cannot fully provide answers to the question of why IS security and crime prevention managers act the way they do without considering the meaning that managers ascribe to their actions and the retail business environments.

IS security and crime prevention management personnel are multicultural professionals from multifaceted backgrounds. Newburn and Webb (1999) argue that the issue of cultural orientation is synonymous with challenges commonly experienced by security managers in preventing business or corporate crimes. Newburn and Webb suggest that one of the major factors that encourages the cultural perception of management in the prevention of crimes is the high degree of internal solidarity and secrecy within the security management. Newburn and Webb (1999) further added that any attempt to curb this influence in business organisations results in cynicism and displeasure. Similarly, Paoline (2003) argues that crime prevention managers develop culturally oriented attitudes, norms and values in relation to their occupation as a means of adapting to the demand of their work and also as a means to cope with the scrutiny of their organisational environment.

Moreover, McConville and Shepherd (1992) discussed cultural orientation regarding security management as an occupational issue which is common in crime prevention settings.

McConville and Shepherd argued that what some lower-level and shop-floor crime prevention managers learn in their occupation is the need to keep their mouths shut about unethical security practices, including those in breach of the security compliance rules, which experienced managers deem necessary in discharging their security management roles and responsibilities. In doing this, Reiner (1992, p. 93) argues that crime prevention managers across all levels tend to adopt secrecy as '*a protective armour shielding them from public knowledge of 'culturally oriented unethical security' infractions*'. And as Newburn and Webb (1999) pointed out earlier, it is not just about secrecy, but about the organisational or occupational level of bureaucracy.

Newburn and Webb added strong bond of loyalty, rated integrity of leadership as other vital features that characterised security professional.

Other sociological studies (e.g.,Van Maanen, 1974; Manning, 1989) argue that crime prevention managers form *culturally oriented unethical* security attitudes, beliefs and values due to their rampant experiences of the challenges associated with their occupation of crime prevention. These studies suggest that those working in a crime prevention setting with limited cultural training and a remit for reassurance are likely to be overwhelmed by the strains associated with crimes prevention. Manning (1989) suggests that there is a link between culture and security practices, which is a huge challenge to security management. This suggestion calls for security managers to watch out for 'contours of the impact of the culture in crimes prevention', especially investigating those aspects of the occupational security cultures undermining compliance with rules/regulations. Slapper and Tombs (1999) argue that preventing corporate business related crimes requires examining the crimes inwardly in terms of organisational culture. Organisations present moral values, which can symbolise the specific organisational identities of their management and employees.

5.6. NEGLIGENCE OF SECURITY CHALLENGES BY RETAIL MANAGEMENT

The implication of cultural influence could nurture the perception of management negligence, which can have a significant impact on prevention of information theft. The culturally oriented unethical practices within the crime prevention management culture has been identified in several reports/inquiries (e.g., Criminal Justice System) as both encouraging inefficiency and hampering security strategies and management efforts in crime prevention (Newburn and Webb, 1999).

Fitzgerald (2007) extends and links the causes of these cultural issues to wider crime prevention challenges which include: inadequacy of educational training of the security managers (especially with regard to culturally oriented unethical security training); abuse of management authority, inadequacy of crime prevention management or poor security management; disregard for honesty and the truth in criminal investigations; contemptuous attitude toward the criminal justice system on the part of the crime prevention manager and rejection of criminal justice system application to crimes prevention.

Moreover, Roukis (2006) suggests that lack of emphasis on the intentions of employees towards ethical security practices could lead to the absence of organisational transparency. Lack of transparent security practices of management can produce criminal behaviour, especially when there are occupational challenges and work pressures are hard on the security management. Roukis (2006) further added that, in the highly challenging occupational environment of crime prevention, a security manager might be tempted to commit internal information theft-related crimes such as thefts of intellectual property, fraudulent manipulation of company stocks and paying bribe to business contractors. Roukis recommends that it is vital to get rid of ambiguity within business environments and to foster cultural-oriented managerial transparency where defined ethical practices are a corporate priority.

In support of Roukis's (2006) recommendation, other researchers (e.g., London, 1999; Dion, 2008) suggest that a 'principled leadership' could be the way for security managers to apply clearly defined culturally oriented ethical business values in their occupational life, such as fairness, honesty, kindness and mutual respect. With principled management integrated with moral courage (use of inner principles to do good regardless of the personal risks), Sekerka and Bagozzi (2007) suggest, managers would be able to make security decisions 'in the light of what is good' for cross-functional management despite personal risks of cultural orientation. Punch (1994) suggests that the impact of cultural orientation on crime prevention can be removed by taking the authority to make decisions out of the hands of top managers. The Criminal Justice Commisssion (1997) recommends that cultural influences can also be reduced by rotating on a regular basis the roles of security managers in 'high risk' or sensitive areas.

5.7. LAW ENFORCEMENT AGENCY AND POLICE INDIFFERENCE

Police indifference is one of the major challenges that affect the security and crime prevention management's effort in preventing internal information theft. This attitude of indifference is rooted in the perception by the police that there are locations or business sectors where crimes are believed to be more prevalent than others. For instance, in the UK, crime reports from cities such as London, Birmingham, Manchester and Glasgow are given priority by the police response team because the cities are seen as sites of notoriety for crimes. If internal information theft incidents reported to the police fell outside these cities, then the police would treat the incidents as '*non-serious*' cases. Berki (1986) refers to this kind of indifference from formal state security officers as '*malevolent indifference*', which can contribute to feelings of insecurity not only on the part of citizens (retail customers) but also on the part of businesses.

Berki (1986, p. 11) explains further that indifference is the disregard meted out to citizens with implied feeling and intention that their interests, desires and security should not count at all and should not be treated in the same way as those of other citizens. This perception that crime reports from smaller cities or small business sectors are disregarded is affecting the police contribution in preventing internal information theft in retail companies. This issue of indifferences in some cases is a misconception, which often leads to negligence on the part of management efforts in preventing internal information theft in online retail (Prenzler, 2009).

This misconception may interfere in some ways with how the law enforcement agency views the crimes in society, which may lead to crime cases from the small cities being neglected to the detriment of the businesses in those cities. Consequently, the incidents of information theft may continue to increase in retail companies unless police change their attitude of indifference to crime investigation and give equal attention to every crime irrespective of the cities or the sectors where the crimes were committed, whether they are high-profile crimes or low-profile crimes.

Police are overwhelmed with the perception that because other crimes are rampant in bigger cities, so too is internal information theft. This perception points to the reason the police believe that information theft-related crimes can be tackled like any other crime. Researchers (e.g., Flanagan, 2008; Rix et al., 2009) argue that police rarely cooperate in investigating information thefts because these crimes emerge from the retail sector, which is a small sector compared to the banking sector. In addition, Ashworth (2005) notes that police would rather get themselves involved with high value or violent crimes. Bamfield (2012) agrees with Ashworth (2005) and argues that although retail crimes such as internal information theft might be important to the police, they may not be one of the top priorities central to their crime prevention strategies and to the policies of police headquarters.

The issue of police indifference in cooperating with retail management in combating information theft might leave the management open to potential litigation for unlawful arrest. This might be the case if a suspected perpetrator was arrested without police cooperation and held for somewhat too long.

The issue of lack of interest shown by police in investigating information theft creates a serious challenge for security managers in retail companies. Walker et al. (2009) argues that police indifference in cooperating with retail managers in combating information theft has greater impact on business organisation than the loss of their business assets. However, Bamfield (2012) suggests that the issue of police indifference lingers in retail companies because the police often criticise retailers' crime prevention policies. In particular, the prevention of crimes (as the case of retail companies) requires specific crime prevention policy changes for retailers to receive substantial police cooperation. This suggestion by Bamfield (2012) supports Seneviratne's (2004) arguments that police should be liable to their own decision whether to adopt a particular policy or prosecute a perpetrator. And that it is the responsibility of police to post their men to crime incidents, but in whatever crime detection and prosecution, police are not servants to anyone, except for the law itself.

Interestingly, these arguments tend to defend police indifference in investigating crimes and also point to the reason behind the attitude of the police regarding their indifference in preventing information theft. In addition, Bamfield (2012) suggests that other issues, such as individual decisions, corporate culture and operational shortages, may contribute to police indifference in preventing information theft in retail companies.

Retail companies are not alone in facing the challenge of police indifference in their effort to prevent information theft.

The Confederation of British Industry (CBI) in their 2010 report (*A Frontline Force: Proposals for More Effective Policing*) suggests that there are concerns about police inefficiency in crime prevention across business sectors. The concerns are worsened by other related issues such as police costs, weak strategic police leadership, inefficiency in their organisational structure and complexity of dealing with crime investigation where police spend lots of time dealing with minor crime cases (Carter, 2003; CBI, 2010; Berry et al., 2011). The Home Office (2011) policy statement (*A New Approach to Crimes*) raised similar concerns about police indifference in preventing crimes.

Comparatively, the CBI's report and the Home Office's policy statements seem to defend the ways things are being done in the police. They argue that the issues of inefficiency and bureaucracy in particular within the police contribute to their attitude of indifference towards crime prevention. Notwithstanding that bureaucracy exists in every institution that deals with crimes (Bamfield, 2012), it is vital that police should have specific ways of dealing with information theft in retail companies. There should be a procedure agreed upon by both retail management and police to minimise the issues of bureaucracy in investigating and prosecuting the internal information theft perpetrators.

Provision of clear roles and responsibilities between the police and retail management would reduce the brick wall that might be encountered by the police during investigation. Clarifying the role of both parties would reduce the amount of time spent on particular information theft incidents. For instance, it could reduce the amount of paperwork regarding internal information theft incidents and witness reports. Consequently, clarifying the roles of the police would reduce the bureaucracy that might have given birth to indifference, which may curb the impact of the internal information in the retail companies. However, this suggestion would work effectively only if there are existing relationships and collaboration between a retail company and the local police. Retail management needs to work collaboratively with the local police. Another option that would change the police indifference in preventing information thefts is to establish a system where the retail security officers and police would work together. This kind of system (*Project Griffin*) was initiated in the case of counter-terrorism where police, business and the private sector security, emergency services and local authorities coordinate to protect UK cities from terrorism (Confederation of European Security Services (CoESS), 2012). There should be police enlistment of retail security officers to enable the retail security management to work collaboratively with them in protecting retail information systems while preventing internal information theft.

Such collaboration ingrained with good relationships would enable the police to understand retail operations, reduce the potential investigation bureaucracy and thus change police indifference in preventing information theft in retail companies.

5.8. OTHER-RELATED CHALLENGES IN PREVENTING INTERNAL INFORMATION THEFT

Both large and small retail companies have most of these key challenges that have been discussed above. Other related challenges are summarised in Figure 5.1 below. The challenges in the upper category of the figure represent the challenges that are recognised as the key issues. These challenges have been the most problematic issues because the demands are much greater for security and crime prevention management in both small and larger retail companies. Comprehensive knowledge of these challenges would provide managers with the right information to make strategies for internal information theft prevention that would be accountable for security/compliance investment probity. These challenges include but are not limited to:

- Clarity of roles
- Management cooperation/support
- Operational changes
- Lack of employees/end-user awareness training
- Lack of clarity of data protection policy
- Lack of trained IS/T staff

- Complexity of internal information theft incidents
- Poor IS/T security tools
- Poor internal data security control and strategy
- Management attitudes towards information theft intervention outcomes

Clarity of Roles: Security and crime prevention management are not clear with the commitment required of them in prevention of internal information theft, although a few pay attention in identifying the vulnerability by classifying the data security cases. Without clear responsibility, the overall internal information theft prevention and internal data security strategies are handicapped. Management should be reflective of what their key roles and responsibilities are in relation to internal information theft prevention. Their roles should not be limited to being busy with routine information theft escalation processes: detection, investigation, etc. They should be more committed to meeting their targets of completing investigation cases while reflecting on the requirement of their job roles.

Management Cooperation/Support: The crime prevention management has difficulty in building effective working relationships with the management of the cross-functional management and local law enforcement agency. This could lead to delays during the crime investigation. Without efficient support between retail management and law enforcement agencies, there may be cases of protracted internal information theft investigations.

The longer the investigation, the more damage the perpetrators would do with the stolen data/information. However, this challenge could be linked to the complex nature of information theft incidents. It is difficult to collaborate with management across businesses and departments when dealing with information theft investigations. Even when implementing best security practices, many retail companies' security managers find it daunting to get support and collaboration of management; it is hard to monitor the best practices across many collaborators because of inter-agency restrictions/policies and privacy-related issues. This is one of the greatest areas of risk for implementing best practices to prevent internal information theft in the context of collaborative management requirements.

Operational changes: There is concern about the issue of operational changes (such as reduction in IT security budgets and shuffling of staff management positions) and the impact on internal information theft prevention in retail companies. This issue is beyond the capability of some security and crime prevention managers. For this reason, they utilise the resources they have at their disposal to implement the latest security tool for prevention of the information theft. The challenge of operational changes in retail companies can lead to other implications, which include the budget constraints, the employees' expertise, and pace of the evolving digital security technologies. For instance, a new security head in some retail companies may argue that deploying and implementing up-to-date security tools is not cheap, insinuating that business owners should spend less. In doing so, the new security manager would be applauded or be recognised for being decisive in his or her spending.

Lack of Employees/End-User Awareness Training: The effort by the management toward training of the employees is established with independent capability in most retail companies. It is either carried out by the human resources or never gets done. In some cases, the attempts to educate all the employees have not yielded the expected result. This setback in employee awareness training on the prevention of internal information theft may be associated with the cost of human resource development.

Moreover, most of the available data security policies are not clear enough to the level of understanding of the shop-floor employees. Even when some retail companies have mandatory e-learning (data protection policy and regulations) that is designed to meet the educational requirements and levels of all management and employees, it may not be. But is this achievable considering the financial implications and other related challenges?

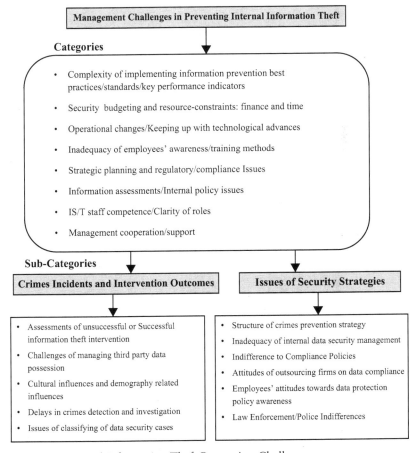

Figure 5.1 Internal Information Theft Prevention Challenges

Lack of clarity of data protection policy: Lack of well-defined policy in retail companies makes it difficult for outsourcing companies to effectively contribute to information theft prevention. Some third-party companies rarely buy in or adhere to the stipulated data security agreement. They handle internal data security with laxity. In most cases, they do not put in place the security checks and measures to avoid any accidental data leakages or theft that might arise during transactions. In some cases, outsourced companies only tick the papers to prove that all the data security checks are up to date, because they never see this as their responsibility—they see it as the responsibility of outsourcing companies to ensure that the data transaction channels are secure. However, where the outsourced companies are not abiding by the data protection policy, most outsourcing companies have resorted to the strategy of coercion and thorough data security auditing. If these strategies failed, outsourcing companies would revoke their business contract with the outsourcing firms. This challenge, in turn, leads to the implication that some retail companies may not have adequate staff expertise and resources for prevention of information theft, and that is the reason for outsourcing security support.

Lack of trained IS/T staff: The instances where the retail companies have to consult outsourcing companies suggest that most of them cannot provide the necessary staff expertise and resources for preventing internal information theft. The practice of outsourcing or hiring an external agent in retail companies may have strained the management effort in establishing the effective cooperation and sharing of responsibilities in regarding effective internal information prevention. This issue extends to other factors in relation to lack of effective communication and role sharing with other complementary management, such as law enforcement agencies. As noted above, the lax attitudes of the outsourcing and law enforcement management in cooperating with retail companies is a major setback. In some cases, outsourced companies' management does not have good knowledge of data security in carrying out their responsibilities in the prevention of internal information theft.

This challenge can lead to delays in information theft investigation protocols because of role clarifications issues, such as *'who does what and where do we go first'*, in the case of internal data security breaches.

Complexity of internal information theft incidents: The complexities of internal information theft incidents, such as the 'seriousness' of the crime, culture, and the outcome of a crime incident, interfere with security strategies. On the issue of incident assessment and interventions, the management often depends on an after-the-fact assessment of intervention processes of typical incidents. They also believe that their experience helped them in designing effective and improved data security strategies. Some information theft interventions may have failed in retail companies because of management that was overly dependent on their experiences in handling their complexities.

Poor IS/T security tools: There are cases in retail companies where security loopholes were discovered within the IT platform and were neglected because management viewed it as not being cost effective to upgrade or as not constituting a high risk. The incidents are rated from high-risk issues to low-risk issues. Perception like this affects the roles of the data security expert in the design of the data security tools, like encryptions for the security of such data.

Poor internal data security control and strategy: Among the top IT security and crime prevention teams, internal data security should be their prime responsibility, but the attitudes of management in retail companies, in some cases, are in a poor state. Although management receives support from cross-management (e.g., HR, software engineering and network/web administrators), there is no collaborative strategy. This issue has led cross-functional teams to place a lot of emphasis on abiding by data security policies but to neglect the key aspect of IT security, which is internal security control.

5.9. SUMMARY OF CHAPTER 5

This chapter has provided insight into challenges that require management attention in the prevention of internal information theft. The challenges vary, as they relate to the complexity of security, the indifference of law enforcement agencies, the cultural orientation of crime prevention managers, and so on. These varying issues weaken implementation of data security strategies in preventing internal information theft. On the other hand, other challenges are interrelated in such a way that one challenge often leads to another. For instance, training of employees is very difficult to achieve in retail companies because of the time and cost. Retail companies may have incentives to invest significant resources in training their IT security and crime prevention employees, but budget constraints and operational changes are still the challenge to deal with.

As a result, they continue to adopt coercive data security approaches which pay off on a short-term basis. However, while internal information theft prevention issues may be an extreme case, the challenges discussed above cannot be considered completely representative or exhaustive prevention challenges faced by management in the retail sector. The purpose of this chapter is not to identify and provide a complete list of internal information theft prevention challenges in retail companies. It is, rather, a guide that can be used as a reference for readers.

To investigate how management can minimise the impact of these prevention challenges, Chapter 6 explores how a strategy of collaborative security management can be effectively deployed in retail companies.

REFERENCES

Ashworth, A. (2005). *Sentencing and Criminal Justice* (4th edn.). Cambridge: Cambridge University Press.
Bamfield, J. (2012). *Shopping and Crime: The Police and Retail Crime*. Basingstoke, UK: Palgrave Macmillan, pp. 180–192.

Berki, R.N. (1986). *Security and Society: Reflections on Law, Order and Politics.* London: J.M. Dent, pp. 11–14.

Berry, G., Briggs P., Erol, R. and van Staden, L. (2011). *The Effectiveness of Partnership Working in a Crime and Disorder Context: A Rapid Evidence Assessment.* Research Report 52. London: The Home Office.

Cain, M. (1973). *Society and the Policeman's Role.* London: Routledge and Kegan Paul.

Cameron, K.S. and Quinn, R.E. (1999). *Diagnosing and Changing Organizational Culture.* Reading, MA: Addison-Wesley.

Carter, P. (2003). *Managing Offenders, Reducing Crime: A New Approach.* London: Home Office.

Chia, P.A., Maynard, S.B. and Ruighaver, A.B. (2003). 'Understanding organisational security culture'. In: M.G. Hunter and K.K. Dhanda (Eds.), *Information Systems: The Challenges of Theory and Practice*, Las Vegas, USA: Information Institute. Available: http://people.eng.unimelb.edu.au/seanbm/research/PacisChia RuighaverMaynard.pdf.

Confederation of British Industry (CBI). (2010). 'A frontline force: Proposals for more effective policing'. *CBI Report on Public Services*, pp. 1–23.

Confederation of European Security Services (CoESS). (2012). *Critical Infrastructure Security and Protection—The Private–Public Opportunity.* Paper and Guidelines by CoESS and Its Working Committee on Critical Infrastructure Protection, May.

Cosgrove, F.M. (2011). *An Appreciative Ethnography of PCSOs in a Northern City.* Doctoral thesis, Northumbria University.

Criminal Justice Commission. (1997). *Integrity in the Queensland Police Service: Implementation and Impact of the Fitzgerald Inquiry Reform.* Brisbane, Australia: Criminal Justice Commission.

Dion, M. (2008). 'Ethical leadership and crime prevention in the organizational setting'. *Journal of Financial Crime*, 15(3), pp. 308–319.

Engel, R.S., Calnon, J.M. and Bernard, T.J. (2002). 'Theory and racial profiling: Shortcomings and future directions in research'. *Justice Quarterly*, 19, pp. 249–273.

Fitzgerald, T. (2007). 'Building management commitment through security councils, or security council critical success factors'. In H. F. Tipton (Ed.), *Information Security Management Handbook.* Hoboken, NJ: Auerbach Publications, pp. 105–121.

Flanagan, R. (2008). 'The review of policing'. *Final Report*, pp. 1–5.

Koh, Ruighaver, A.B., Maynard, S.B. and Ahmad, A. (2005). 'Security governance: Its impact on security culture'. Proceedings of 3rd Australian Information Security Management Conference, pp. 47–56.

London, M. (1999). 'Principled leadership and business diplomacy: A practical, values-based direction for management development'. *The Journal of Management Development*, 18(2), pp. 170–89.

Manning, P.K. (1989). 'Occupational culture'. In W.G. Bayley (Ed.), *The Encyclopaedia of Police Science.* New York: Garfield, p. 362.

Manning, P.K. (1995). 'The study of policing'. *Policing and Society*, 8(1), pp. 23–43.

Maynard, S.B. and Ruighaver, A.B. (2006). 'What makes a good information security policy: A preliminary framework for evaluating security policy quality'. Proceedings of the fifth annual security conference, Las Vegas, Nevada, USA.

McConville, M. and Shepherd, D. (1992). *Watching Police, Watching Communities*. London: Routledge.

Newburn, T. and Webb, B. (1999). 'Understanding and preventing police corruption: Lessons from the literature', *Home Office Policing and Reducing Crime Unit Research and Reducing Crime Unit*. Police Research Series, pp. 1–45.

Paoline, E.A. (2003). 'Taking stock: Toward a richer understanding of police culture'. *Journal of Criminal Justice*, 31(2003), pp. 199–214.

Popa, M. and Doinea, M. (2007). 'Audit characteristics for information systems'. *Revista Informatica Economic* , 4(44), pp. 103–106.

Prenzler, T. (2009). *Police Corruption: Preventing Misconduct and Maintaining Integrity: Advance in Police Theory and Practice Series* (2nd edn.). CRC Press; Taylor and Francis, pp. 15–25. Available: https://www.crcpress. com/Police-Corruption-Preventing-Misconduct-and-Maintaining-Integrity/ Prenzler/9781420077964.

PriceWaterCoopers (PWC). (2014). 'Information Security Breach Survey (ISBS) technical report'. Available: https://www.gov.uk/government/uploads/system/uploads /attachment_data/file/307296/bis-14–767-information-security-breaches-survey-2014-technical-report-revision1.pdf, Accessed 2 April 2014.

Punch, M. (1996). *Dirty Business: Exploring Corporate Misconduct*. London: Sage.

Reiner, R. (1992). *The Politics of the Police*. Hemel Hempstead, UK: Harvester Wheatsheaf.

Rix, A., Joshua, F. and Maguire, M. (2009). *Improving Public Confidence in the Police: A Review of the Evidence* (2nd edn.). Home Office Research Report 28. London: Home Office, pp. 1–4.

Roukis, G.S. (2006). 'Globalisation, organizational opaqueness, and conspiracy'. *Journal of Management Development*, 25(10), pp. 970–980.

Sanders, A. and Young, R. (2003). 'Police powers' in: T. Newburn (Ed.), *Handbook of Policing*. Cullompton, UK: Willan Publishing, pp. 281–312.

Scerra, N. (2011). 'Impact of police cultural knowledge on violent serial crime investigation'. *Policing: An International Journal of Police Strategies and Management*, 34(1), pp. 83–96.

Sekerka, L.E. and Bagozzi, R.P. (2007). 'Moral courage in the workplace: moving to and from the desire and decision to act'. *Business Ethics: A European Review*, 16(2), pp. 132–149.

Seneviratne, M. (2004). 'Policing the police in the United Kingdom'. *Policing & Society*, 14(4), pp. 329–347.

Skolnick, J. (1966). *Justice Without Trial: Law Enforcement in Democratic Society*. New York: Macmillan College Division.

Slapper, G. and Tombs, S. (1999). *Corporate Crime*. Harlow: Longman Criminology Series, Pearson Education Ltd.

Tsai, J.L. (2001). 'Cultural orientation of Hmong young adults'. *Journal of Human Behaviour and the Social Environment*, 3(4), pp. 99–114.

Van Maanen, J. (1974). 'Working the street: A developmental view of police behaviour'. In H. Jacob (Ed.), *The Potential for Reform of Criminal Justice. Sage Criminal Justice System Annual Review, 3*. Thousand Oaks, CA: Sage.

Waddington, P.A.J. (1999a). *Policing Citizens: Authority and Rights*. London: Routledge.

Westley, W. (1970). *Violence and the Police*. Cambridge, MA: The Free Press.

6 Collaborative Internal Information Theft Prevention
Towards Innovative Security

6.1. INTRODUCTION

The need for security and crime prevention management to work collaboratively in updating security tools has been identified to have a huge impact on information theft prevention. In recent years, advances (e.g., Internet Engineering Task Force, Keeping Internet Routing Secure, Mutually Agreed Norms for Routing Security, etc.) in the use of computer technology have provided significant opportunity for collaboration in the crime and security decision-making process. The concept of collaboration provides strategies required to integrate cross-functional management and their tasks in retail operation. However, for the technology to have a significant impact on crime prevention, human, institutional and organisational barriers (identified in Chapter 5) need to be eliminated (Gilling, 2009). The collaborative approach streamlines IS security practices by dynamically helping management to create and align essential roles to eliminate potential management conflicts in their effort to prevent internal information theft in retail businesses.

As defined by Wenger et al. (2002), practice refers to the knowledge and the competencies of members, as well as to the specific things that they do. 'Members' in this guide refers to the security and crime prevention management. Interestingly, there are few or no books on the 'actual practical guide' for internal information theft prevention. The 'practice' of information theft prevention management has been a contested terrain, unsettled in the minds of security and crime prevention management, academics and policy makers (Wenger, 1998). This chapter will, as far as is possible within the confines of this guide, put together the 'best practices' of information theft prevention and develop a framework for how they can be applied together by management in retail companies.

6.2. ATTRIBUTES OF COLLABORATIVE INFORMATION THEFT PREVENTION

The collaborative concept in prevention of internal information theft needs to be embedded with essential elements for its effective implementation.

These elements are basic structures that would enhance management workflows in relation to security and crime prevention practices in preventing internal information theft. The three essential attributes for effective crime prevention and security management collaboration are:

- Agility,
- Interoperability, and
- Vigilance.

Agility: Both the security and crime prevention management need to be agile, responsive and available to enable adaptive planning and delivery of IS/T security roles. This attribute would encourage evolutionary, flexible and rapid response to change in evolving information theft trends in retail businesses. It would enable IS security management to prevent known risks, and provide a platform for effective responses to potential security loopholes.

Vigilance: Security strategies should be designed to provide management with the capability to integrate security intelligence to anticipate data security threats. This attribute would enable the management to evaluate risks and make informed decisions; enhance the adoption and collaboration of role sharing concepts; and to balance the technical controls with a process for applying security to employees, partners and third parties that contributes to internal information theft prevention.

Interoperability: By adopting the people, process and technology (PPT) approach, IS security management becomes a single system with the unified goal of internal information prevention. The collaborative role allows for easier monitoring and measurements. Importantly, it would give management control, which would minimise the impact of benign mistakes from employees' actions and on processes related to internal information theft-related risks.

6.3. COLLABORATIVE SECURITY MANAGEMENT: A ROLE-BASED FRAMEWORK (RBF)

This framework is conceptualised as a role-based framework (RBF). It incorporates internal information theft prevention practices recommended by IS security management from various business contexts. The prevention practices in this context are a set of documents, frameworks, ideas, information, languages, stories, styles and tools that both the security and crime prevention management share. Gercke et al. (2011) suggest that the cross-functional partnership that incorporates interdependent coordination of roles with skill sharing is the most effective prevention practice in any areas of information theft-related crimes. This suggestion could be practicable only in a defined business operation, online retail in this context, which may enable understanding of the issues of internal information theft.

Sharing of roles in relation to prevention of information theft is required in order to encourage leveraging, expanding of skills as appropriate, and support for external relationships with agencies. Role sharing brings together expertise from diverse management backgrounds, HR, law enforcement, and IS security. Each management background holds information linked to IS security, which, if shared, can provide comprehensive prevention views of criminal activity. This, in most cases, can be evidence-based practice. When these practices are based on equal sharing, an equal level of power, mutual respect and understanding, then the prevention strategies are implementable. This collaborative concept emphasises that information theft prevention should not be mere technological fixes but integrated IS/T security strategies—which are explicitly or implicitly held by practitioners.

It is important for security and crime prevention management to work together to harmonise common strategies for internal information prevention in businesses, primarily, to reduce the complexity in their analysis and application. Although some information theft prevention practices and frameworks have attempted to clarify their contextual analysis, as discussed in Chapter 4, the use of the concept of collaborative management has sought to provide clear role-based concepts of what could and should be implemented.

This concept of RBF underpins the suggestions of scholars and, more importantly, of practitioners' need to increasingly work in information theft prevention. Ekblom (2010) and Sarnecki (2005), proponents of the intra-organisational management integration that underpins the theoretical analysis of collaborative security management, did not view their suggestions as being solely about improving the interaction of management roles in their business environments in relation to crime prevention. In particular, Ekblom (2010) suggests that numerous conceptualisations of crime prevention practices and theories delineate the degree to which it might be applied by the management.

The need for change in the paradigm of information theft prevention that was identified in Chapter 4—the shift from software-based and generic models of information theft prevention to analysis of the integration of shared management roles—is attempted to be bridged with this concept of role-based framework (RBF). This analysis of the role integration approach is important in this guide, as it is through this new framework that management can be enlightened and prepared to tackle emerging security threats in retail operation. Thus, understanding of the attributes of RBF and the diffusion of the responsibility for internal information theft prevention beyond either software-based or generic models is an explicit critique of the very idea of collaborative crime prevention and security management.

6.3.1. The Key Attributes of the Role-Based Framework

The four key attributes of the role-based framework are synthesised to ensure that management efforts and strategies are directed toward effective internal information theft prevention. The key attributes include:

- Collaborative role-based monitoring;
- Support capabilities;

- Service-level agreements;
- Flexible support.

Collaborative role-based monitoring: Collaboration between security and crime prevention management provides continuum and optimum roles/ responsibilities across functional management team from the foundation and is proactive to prevent information theft risks;

Foundation: IS/T security warranty and remote support to law enforcements and outsourcing companies, and establishes their requirements with respect to service line agreements;

Preventive: Multi-management IS/T security support, clearly defined roles at the respective management level, dynamic and available management support.

Support capabilities: Collaborative security improves both the effectiveness and efficiency of IT/S maintenance and support. It provides opportunities for the Information security management systems (ISMS) to leverage the competency and best results which may come from out-tasking the cross-functions to strengthen IS/T security strategy. It makes it possible for an informed, effective maintenance and technical expertise to be shared in a dynamic process.

Service-level agreements: RBF is a customisable schema at hierarchical management levels to meet business information security management system budgets, needs and strategies.

This means that service-level agreements (SLAs) can now be linked dynamically to shifting roles, responsibilities and workloads. Rather than being defined by static roles that do not reflect changing internal information security demands, the internal information theft prevention service level can fluctuate in response to internal security risks; meets businesses' expectations for real-time role-oriented information security management; assures data security processes and business continuity through clear management roles.

Flexible Support: Collaborative security help (information security management systems) ISMS to accomplish complex internal security tasks, manage or out-task IS/T security. It provides flexible knowledge transfer to address a range of information theft prevention complexities that might be beyond the expertise of management support. It provides the option to choose management roles and services that better suit the business data security operation and structure; creates information security optimised maintenance and dynamic prevention; minimises the ISMS service and roles that seem to clash; provides integrated information security service management, optimisation, and flexible delivery choices and leverages the expertise of cross-functional management to reduce the cost of IS platform as a service (PaaS) and infrastructure as a service (IaaS).

Collaborative management enhances implementation of prevention strategies to create structure that can help to effectively deliver the following retail business security objectives:

- Internal information theft prevention policy design and implementation,
- Encourage best practice to minimise internal information theft risks,

- Maximise internal security performance, and
- Align management roles and responsibilities

6.3.2. Structure of Role-Based Framework

The knowledge of collaborative information theft prevention requires that management should be designed as the body that encompasses complementary management team members—crime prevention, IT security, human resources and law enforcement agency. It classifies management roles in a hierarchical level from the top management to the front line management. It follows the stages of crime prevention processes, which include intervention, intelligence, implementation, collaboration and remediation measures. Intervention in this context refers to a combination of internal information prevention strategies designed to change or improve the employees' behaviour or perception towards information theft. The elements of intervention include but are not limited to information theft prevention awareness training, data protection training, information theft incident reporting and whistle blowing.

These elements can contribute immensely by promoting employee support, influencing their IS security knowledge and skills, and creating supportive working environments, policies and resources. Intelligence is referred to as operations undertaken by IS security and crime prevention management to gather information that provides a better understanding of internal information theft characteristics—causes and methods of propagation (Karn, 2013). Remediation measures in relation to information theft prevention are the actions that management takes to correct the damage done by perpetrators.

In this guide, it is effective implementation and efficient collaboration by the management that can minimise the chance for a remediation process. While implementation is the translation of the chosen IS security strategy into action to achieve information theft prevention goals and objectives, collaboration is the key for achieving it. Hence, collaborative security management defines working together towards a goal of preventing information theft (Gercke et al., 2011).

Collaborative security management can be either inter-organisational, when it involves external agents (e.g., law enforcements, partners, outsourcing companies), or intra-organisational, when the roles of security and crime prevention managers are shared within the same organisation. Intra- and inter-organisation collaboration in preventing information theft can affect the effectiveness of IS security strategies in retail businesses. The impact can be significant on information theft prevention strategies such as information security policy, employee information theft awareness programmes, consumer data protection, identity management, law enforcement, employees training, reporting procedures, data compliance management and victims support.

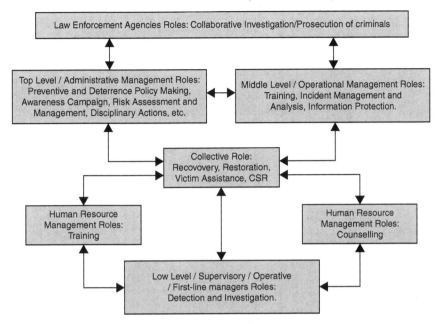

Figure 6.1 Structure of Role-Based Framework

6.3.3. Role-Based Information Theft Prevention: Cross-Functional Management

To ensure that the impact of collaborative security management is significant in every aspect of internal information prevention strategies, RBF should be organised, as shown in Figure 6.1 above, as a sequence of management levels which emphasise the clarification of roles—IS/T security, IS audit, crime prevention, HR and law enforcement. The arrows, as shown in the figure, depict the interdependence of shared roles through monitoring, reporting, and collaboration between management levels. The roles identified in this figure have their foundations in criminology (crime deterrence theory, Pearson theory and Cressey's fraud triangle theory), IS and management perspective (policy and risk management) and sociology (staff fraud, white collar crimes and corporate frauds).

6.3.3.1. Top Management

The role of the top-level management for prevention of internal information theft includes making preventive and deterrent policies, risk assessment and management, disciplinary actions, etc. An effective information theft prevention policy within any business organisation is a necessary first step towards the development of strategic information security for integrated management. The policy should also include other components, such as definitive objectives, assumptions and directives which could increase the possibilities of discovery or decrease the probability of committing information theft in the organisation. There should be policy guides, clear procedures and internal rules for reporting and investigating cases of identity theft. Good policy statements are the basis for other steps to be built upon. Without prudent policy from the management of the organisation, other steps like risk assessment and management would not be effective.

Top managers should play hands-on roles in ensuring effective information protection, detection of fraud, investigations and incident management, so that prevention policies are taken seriously by all levels of an organisation. In doing so, their front-line experience would help them to develop more effective policies.

6.3.3.2. Middle Management
The middle-level management in a typical retail company comprises departmental heads and regional managers, etc. They are answerable to the top-level management for functioning of their departments/teams while ensuring organising and directing roles, which include training, incident management and analysis and information protection. They implement the organisational goals, objectives and plans according to the directions/policies of the top management. They should be able to clarify and explain internal information theft deterrent policies and guidelines from the top management to lower level management, thus acting as a mediator between the two levels. The governing policies discussed above are supported by the technical policies, thus they cover most rules and regulations in more detail by adding to these rules the areas that are relevant to the technology. These policies are meant for the technical custodians, as they carry out routine security responsibilities within the business.

The system and database administrators need to be kept abreast of the current technical policies within and outside the retail domain. As internal fraud threats are becoming more dynamic, with fraudsters continuing to devise new techniques to exploit the easiest target, crime specialists suggested that retail industry should continue to invest in systems and controls to avoid being targeted as the weakest link (Financial Crime and Service Authority, 2009). The advancement in the use of information technology has enabled criminals to continue to refine and update their techniques.

However, some of the new complex technologies that have been noted to have proven data and information security are biometric technologies, cryptography, authentication and certification and single sign-on technologies. It has been proven that a combination of these technologies built on a well designed and enforced set of security rules and regulations always deters internal criminals from fraud (Schneier, 2004).

Nevertheless, technical employees should know the technical guidelines and policies, along with the effective application of the security software, to increase their likelihood of preventing cases of information theft in online retail. Guidelines are procedural document lists and strategies adopted by business organisations. In most retail companies, the guidelines are developed based on the policy of the individual department. Employees pay less attention to these guidelines perhaps because of the light consequences of their violations. More attention should be given to the preventive guidelines on information theft prevention and other common data recovery plan guidelines. The management at this level should be responsible for the coordination of different aspects, such as the training of staff, incident management and rule-enforcement policies and guidelines.

The training of the employees in areas of information protection and data security should be their priority. They can organise seminars for the training of employees, while ensuring effective incident management and analysis. This involves the management and analysis of the aftermath of identity fraud occurrences. The ability of the companies to implement rigorous incident management procedures relies heavily on the effectiveness of the middle management. Without such cooperation of the middle management and top management, information theft would be difficult to manage.

6.3.3.3. Supervisory Management

Also known as the first-line management, supervisory management usually consists of store managers, shift supervisors, foreperson and team leaders. Their basic role is the supervision of everyday business operations. Since first-line managers have a strong influence over the employees and interact with them on a daily basis, they can play a vital role in the detection and investigation of identity theft related crimes. The major problem facing investigation of these crimes still boils down to lack of clarity of responsibility and less interaction or flow of communication between management and employees, thus making cases of internal information theft difficult to prove when the perpetrators are caught. Supervisors can help address this problem by facilitating constant communication with employees.

6.3.3.4. Roles of Human Resource Management

One of the most effective ways to mitigate the threat of internal information theft schemes (e.g., collusion and coercion) is for human resource managers to raise the level of awareness among all employees. It is important to let all the employees know the consequences of colluding or involving themselves in any form of internal identity related crimes. Organisations, through human resources, need to ensure that staff members are aware of where to report the cases of fraudulent activities within the organisations. There should also be the provision for the employees to feel confident that the matter would be treated professionally. Based on this consideration that the role of human resource management is very vital in prevention of information theft, the structure of RBF (see Figure 6.1 above) depicts two loops in which the top and the middle level management roles and responsibilities are hinged.

6.3.3.5. Roles of Law Enforcement Agencies

These are agencies that have a vital role to play in retail operations, as they may have essential access to employees and skills to tackle internal information theft cases beyond the reporting of incidents. Outsourcing specialist teams to deal with these crimes is recommended. They can also play a major role in educating businesses on best practices for effective internal information prevention measures. Retail managements can assist law enforcement and regulatory authorities in the fight against internal employee fraud by providing them with vital information regarding business organisations, given that taking legal action against the fraudster might be expensive and also an effective deterrent for others (ACAS, 2008). It is the role of retail management to create awareness of policies of data protection and the role of law enforcement agencies to enforce the policies. The policy for prevention of information theft in retail industry should include these purposes:

- Protection of stakeholders and information;
- Set of rules for expected behaviour of employees, management, system administrators, security personnel, and users;
- Authorise and define the consequences of violation of rules, authorise security personnel to investigate, monitor and probe;
- Help to minimise security risks, define industry consensus stance on information and data security.

These policies and legislations can be deployed and made available across management, technical and employees' levels. In addition, other governing policies, technical policies and guidelines should be adapted to cover information and related proprietary data security. In doing so, the government data protection data and other important legislations should also be incorporated into the overall company's security policy.

However, in the UK, for instance, some retail companies still neglect the integration of the government's data protection acts, such as the Data Protection Act (1998), Freedom of Information 2000, and Computer Misuse Act 1990. Sommer (2012) has advised that raising awareness among all employees about this relevant legislation relating to data security has proved to be one of the effective ways to mitigate the threat of information theft in businesses.

6.3.3.6. Collective Roles

The employees and stakeholders in online retail are expected to make more than just economic contributions. Both parties need to see and begin to recognise their responsibility to secure and promote information management in their companies (Listermann and Romesberg, 2009). This responsibility should not be limited to the level required by law, but should extend to protection of identity proprietary information in order to achieve secure retail business operations. The application of the concepts of Corporate Social Responsibility (CSR) in the context of prevention of internal information theft in retail information systems security is still scarce in practice. Although CSR has been applied extensively in many business sectors, retail information security management in particular is still behind (Tsiakis, 2009). The Basel Committee on Banking Supervision encourages senior management to promote their organisational culture by exemplary life through integrity. There is a need for online retail companies to stress the importance of trust between the managers and employees. This would assist in monitoring employees' suspicious lifestyles, which may pose potential detrimental effects to both the employee and employer. Intelligence agencies and top human resource managers have listed various policies which could create a desired culture in every organisation.

Some of these include fraud management policy, employee fraud prevention policy, code of conduct or business ethics, disciplinary policy, fraud reporting policy whistle blowing policy, staff assistance policy and fraud specialist policy, etc.

Prevention of internal information theft in retail companies can also be provided through a company's CSR—a voluntary commitment to internalise in corporate pivotal decisions and strategy practices that contribute to social development. There is need for the security managers to incorporate CSR activities into a corporate strategy of information security practices. Lewis (2006) suggests that incorporation of motivation in the workplace for the employees who promote honesty has contributed towards the development of ethical company cultures, which in turn reduces the cases of information theft in retail businesses.

6.4. SUMMARY OF CHAPTER 6

This chapter has provided knowledge on how collaborative security and crime prevention management can be structured to maximise the management roles in the prevention of internal information theft. As earlier discussed in Chapter 5, the orientation of management in relation to the organisational culture of retail companies may not be separated from the security management. For an effective prevention of internal information theft in retail companies, there is a need for change in the cultural orientation from independent security to collaborative security. Braithwaithe (1989) suggests that the increased emphasis on collaborative managerial responsibility embedded in an understanding of cultural influence aimed at ensuring compliance is more likely to have long-lasting benefits in preventing corporate or business crimes than other deterrence measures.

Based on this argument, Dahler-Larsen (1997) concludes that all the management and employees have their 'share' of responsibilities to play in the way their operations justify their decisions and actions regarding security and crime prevention practices.

The knowledge of collaborative management on the prevention of internal information theft in retail companies would equip security and crime prevention managers with a valuable tool in managing the multicultural dimension of the management work force. This knowledge would also equip the management to develop a strategic cross-functional and socio-cultural skills needed for preventing and investigating internal information theft incidents. However, management role sharing can be affected by a number of factors, including people, operations, processes, organisational roles, and technology and management characteristics. These factors can be relevant to the success of information systems (IS) security in organisations. If there is clarity of roles by the management, then the adoption of collaborative management can be beneficial to retail companies. The ways of improving collaborative management strategies can be simplified by asking these key questions:

i. What are the key roles that can clearly impact security management performance in the prevention of internal information theft?
ii. What practices are likely to improve collaborative management between security and crime prevention in the prevention of information theft?

Attempts to answer these questions would provide insights into the applicability of collaborative management in the prevention of internal information theft. The next discussion, in Chapter 7, provides knowledge of the practical application of collaborative management in the case of data compliance audits of selected companies in the UK.

REFERENCES

ACAS. (2008). 'Advisory handbook: Discipline and grievances at work'. Available: http://www.acas.org.uk/media/pdf/s/o/Acas-Guide-on-discipline-and grievances_at_work _(April_11)-accessible-version-may-2012.pdf, Accessed 7 December 2011.

Braithwaite, J. (1989). *Crime, Shame and Reintegration.* Cambridge: Cambridge University Press.

Dahler-Larsen, P. (1997). Organizational Identity as "Crowded Category": A Case of Multiple and Quickly Shifting We-typifications. In: Sackmann, S. (ed.): Cultural Complexity in Organizations (p. 367–90). Thousand Oaks: Sage.

Data Protection Act. (1998). 'Part VI (Miscellaneous and General), Section 55, Office of Public Sector Information'. Available: http://www.legislation.gov.uk/ukpga/1998/29/ section/4, Accessed 14 January 2014.

Ekblom, P. (2010). *Crime Prevention, Security and Community Safety with the 5Is Framework.* Basingstoke, UK: Palgrave Macmillan.

Financial Crime and Service Authority (FCSA). (2009). 'Consumer Financial Education: Money Made Clear'.

Gercke, M., de Almeida, G.M., Lawson, P., Callanan, C. and Simion, R. (2011). *Handbook on Identity Theft Related Crimes* (3rd edn.). United Nations Office on Drugs and Crimes, Vienna, Publishing and Library Section, pp. 107–169.

Gilling, D.J. (2009). Multi-Agency Crime Prevention: Some Barriers to Collaboration, *The Howard Journal of Criminal Justice*, 33(3), pp.246–257.

Karn, J. (2013). 'Policing and crime reduction: The evidence and its implications for practice'. Police Effectiveness in a Changing World Project, pp. 1–36. Available: http://www.police-foundation.org.uk/uploads/catalogerfiles/policing-and-crime-reduction/police-foundation-police-effectiveness-report.pdf, Accessed 24 June 2014.

Lewis, G. (2006). *Organisational Crisis Management: The Human Factor*, Auerbach Publications-Taylor and Francis Group: Boca Raton, New York.

Listerman, R.A. and Romesberg, J. (2009). 'Creating a culture of security is key to stopping a data breach. Are we safe yet?' *Strategic Finance*, pp. 27–33.

Sarnecki, J. (2005). 'Knowledge-based crime prevention, theoretical points of departure for practical crime prevention'. Paper presented at the Eleventh United Nations Congress on Crime Prevention and Criminal Justice, 18–25 April 2005, Bangkok, Thailand, pp. 1–11.

Schneier, B. (2004). *Secrets and Lies: Digital Security in a Networked*. Hoboken, NJ: John Wiley and Sons, p. 432.

Sommer, P. (2012). *Digital Evidence, Digital Investigations and E-Disclosure: A Guide to Forensic Readiness for Organisations, Security Advisers and Lawyers* (3rd edn.). London: Information Assurance Advisory Council.

Tsiakis, T. (2009). 'Contribution of corporate social responsibility to information security management'. *Information Security Technical Report*, 14(4), pp. 217–222.

Wenger, E. (1998). *Communities of Practice: Learning, Meaning, and Identity*. Cambridge: Cambridge University Press.

Wenger, E., McDermott, R. and Snyder, W. (2002). *Cultivating Communities of Practice: A Guide to Managing Knowledge*. Boston: Harvard Business School Press.

7 Application of Collaborative Management in Information Theft Prevention

7.1. INTRODUCTION

This chapter presents results of cross-case analysis in selected UK retail companies, adapted from Okeke (2015), to show the benefits of collaborative management while conducting information security audit (ISA) while preventing internal information theft. The approach of the collaborative audit has only enhanced the audit plan, criteria, scope and duration; it has also improved the audit report, efficiency and effectiveness of the audit operations in compliance with regulations. The case results provided in this chapter acknowledge that the collaborative ISA approach enhances the management effort in building a strong work ethic in prevention of internal information theft. And this can be evidenced by security management performance in meeting the information security requirement in prevention of information theft. In addition, the collaborative ISA approach can enable retail security audit teams to detect loopholes in their IT security systems and tackle them effectively and collaboratively.

A collaborative management effort could provide an effective internal security control and improved risk assessment against internal threats. If management can collectively take control of internal IS security issues, it would ease the ISA procedures, reduce the audit time and cut down logistics. The collaborative ISA approach can also promote the sharing of security expertise and IT skills that can contribute to effective ISA in prevention of information theft. It is vital to note that collaborative ISA can enhance the chance to identify internal security risks, which can be achieved through effective collaboration between audit and IT security management.

In contrast, in the cases where the audit practices and management roles were not collaborative, like in the case of an independent audit, the impact of ISA on information theft prevention may not be realised. Collaboration can make it possible for management to share their roles/responsibilities, thereby improving the likelihood for security and crime prevention management to achieve effective security implementations. The effective information security audit in relation to prevention of information theft may depend on collaboration of management effort and roles. Thus, it is required that the management efforts and roles among the IT security and crime prevention management should be shared to achieve the goal of effective security against information theft in retail companies.

7.2 BENEFITS OF COLLABORATIVE INFORMATION SECURITY AUDIT

The benefits of Information Security Audit (ISA) can be measured based on three key criteria: time, logistics and effectiveness. Cost reduction and internal security control have been identified as the major impacts of using collaborative ISA approaches in the prevention of information theft.

Cost reduction benefits: The use of independent first-party audit and second-party audits could be perceived by retail management as cost saving if a retail company is paying for a few audit teams. However, subjectively, such companies may incur the indirect costs of a protracted audit and potential security risks compared to an approach where both first-party and second-party audits are working together. In this collaborative audit by a first party and a second party, both audit teams would utilise the combined support of IT security, a security auditor and an external auditor to ease the burden of audit roles and responsibilities.

The approach of combined support would enable the team to prepare the audit plan in advance to meet the audit criteria and expected targets. The collaborative atmosphere would facilitate the audit performance and provide room for suggestions and new requirements.

Benefits of internal security control assurance: A sound internal security control is one of the benefits of collaborative security management. Independent audits through either first-party audit or second-party audit can create bias between retail companies and the visiting auditor. And this might extend the audit duration and more cost to business, not only for the cost of the security auditing but also the cost of disrupting business operation during the audit. Using a collaborative audit approach pays in reducing the internal information theft risk, as it gives the audit team the opportunity to leverage their skills. In a case where the software engineer is part of the collaborative management, it would be helpful for the team to review and meet the requirements of installing the latest updates needed to mitigate internal security threats.

Information systems security knowledge: The sharing of expertise between the IT security support and internal auditor can create a strong internal IS control system. This can facilitate comprehensive scrutiny of security risks and flaws and an opportunity to collaboratively design strategies for resolving the risks. This practice enables both the external and internal auditor to work cooperatively and in a timely fashion to resolve potential internal information theft issues. It can enable the audit team to avoid poor security audit planning, inconsistencies and shifting of responsibilities. These issues have great impact in meeting the aims and objectives of the ISA.

7.3. MANAGEMENT COLLABORATION BEFITS EFFECTIVE ISA IMPLEMENTATION

Retail companies with greater collaboration of management roles are more likely to have effective implementation of IS security strategies required for the prevention of internal information theft. Management with shared understanding of data security operations are more likely to achieve a better security strategy in prevention of internal information theft; Management collaborative role sharing is likely to affect the level of performance management in preventing internal information theft.

Some retail companies neglect collaborative approaches in implementing security audit practices across their operations, as well as process and technologies. Some management take sharing of the prevention practices for granted and manage information theft prevention in relatively independent and predictable ways across their operations. In particular, the case analysis by Okeke (2015) suggests that it is vital for security management to share their data security roles and practices within the operational environment. The empirical evidence from Okeke (2015) shows that companies that neglect utilising IS management collaborative capabilities often encounter the challenges identified in Chapter 5.

7.3.1 Implications of Collaboration in Internal Information Theft Prevention

One of the consequences of lack of collaboration in the implementation of internal information theft prevention practices is a misunderstanding of IT security terms. The effect of this misunderstanding can lead to a breakdown and management override. There could be a situation in which the internal auditor is protective and shifting the responsibility to the company's top management.

For instance, the internal auditor may not resolve issues related to security risks; instead, the risks would be left as the responsibility of the head of security management. In some cases, there would be a complete breakdown in communication among the audit team because of their independent work. This analysis agreed with Potter and Waterfall's (2012) PWC ISBS report, which found that more than 56 per cent of business managers do not work together with their information security auditors. Instead, they leave the responsibility to the information security auditors or rather rely on the contingency plans, with the sole intention of cutting cost or investing less on IT maintenance. This issue was also noted by Potter and Waterfall (2012), who reported that less than half of large companies and only a quarter of small ones are collaboratively measuring the coordination of their regulatory data compliance and security management.

Moreover, this issue of the perception of ISA costs corresponds to the suggestions of Chris Potter of PWC ISBS (2012) that most managers often fail to evaluate their ISA investment. In line with the benefits of the collaborative ISA approach, discussed above, the first-party audit seems to pay off when an external auditor is hired, but, apparently, the cost of the expended time for the audit and poor audit execution outweigh the benefits of the approach. The operation manager may fail to evaluate the pros and cons of paying for the external IS security auditor. This observation confirms Cilli's (2003) suggestion that IS retail management fail to provide answers to ISA effectiveness and efficiency related questions such as IS security awareness, control, profiling and performance measurement. According to Nieminski (2008), effective internal control management equips the ISA team to detect, correct and prevent related information theft threats. She further suggested that any crack in the internal control management of the ISA team often leads to limited judgement, breakdowns and management override.

Another notable implication of lack of collaboration of management in implementing effective prevention practices is that companies are likely to develop data security practices that align with the internal information theft prevention challenges they face. Because such practices lead to the perception of improved IS security, the management may begin to take the challenges for granted. This perception would lead to the development of culturally unethical security practices among the management. Consequently, it then leads to development of internalised prevention practices that are difficult to change. The external auditor may work with the available IS resources and information at their disposal to justify the cost of the services being paid for. This observation agrees with the suggestions of ACFE (2012) and ISBS (2012) that the perceived high cost of data compliance management and the assumption that adequate security checks are already in place often contribute to defects in the internal data security of most retail companies.

In order for crime prevention managers to deliver and counter this challenge of culturally oriented unethical security practices, Innes (2003) suggests that crime prevention managers must be integrated into an ethical occupational and organisational culture. This suggestion reaffirms the proposal of the role-based framework that effective integration of a cross-functional management team can enhance management performance in preventing internal information theft. In order to support the integration and execute the roles of their work efficiently, this suggestion requires that management will endorse the ethical cultural attitudes, beliefs and values to which they are exposed. In other words, the management will have to construct ethical cultural meanings that reflect their occupational responsibilities that are compliant with information theft prevention practices. However, this commitment to internal information theft prevention might not work for all cases. Strict compliance with the rules of security may encourage managers not to believe in themselves or not to follow their instinct in managing information theft incidents they deem suspicious.

An attempt to abide by strict compliance rules may make managers to have shared understanding to comply with security rules and to avoid scrutiny from their top managers. The shared understanding between the security managers would be focused on their occupational goal of 'getting the job done', avoiding criticism from the top managers by sticking to the clear security rules of the shared culture. This perception is what Van Maanen (1974) calls 'cover your ass', a characteristic of the security culture, which means that the security managers would make a conceivable story— that is, the security managers would make a conceivable story to cover them for everything they do when they are on duty in the name of abiding by culturally oriented security practices and security compliance rules.

7.3.2 Recommendations for Effective Collaboration

The discussion of the implications of collaborative management indicates that there is a strong need for retail companies to change their security strategy from an independent approach to a collaborative security approach. Importantly, the major change should be the review of the existing security culture, policies, procedures, structures and systems. Previous studies (e.g., McDonald and Nijhof, 1999; Roukis, 2006; Sekerka and Bagozzi, 2007) argue that implementing an effective ethics programme in an organisation would make the management and employees aware of formal organisational goals, information theft prevention, in this case, and their informal norms. Pelletier and Bligh (2006) recommends that business organisations should have suitable procedures and systems for ethical decision-making regarding sharing their employee roles and responsibilities. This suggestion corresponds with the recommendation of this guide that establishing a collaborative management system would enhance the necessary skills for ethical practices in retail companies.

Moreover, there is need for retail companies to invest in a collaborative management approach to the prevention of internal information theft. This practice can improve the overall effectiveness and reduce the impact of the identified challenges of online retail companies in the implementation of effective security systems. Additional benefits may accrue from these practices when supplemented with collaborative ISA by the management. However, the benefits might depend on the level of IT skills of the management, the perception of management roles, top management support and the organisational operations. The analysis of the implications above has shown that collaborative management can enhance the likelihood of effective and strategic prevention of information theft. It suggests that a collaborative approach where internal and external auditors work together can be a more robust audit practice than first/second party audit that entails either an internal or external auditor.

The collaborative approach is more effective in putting a check on the internal control of IS in retail company. This practice would enable the data security audit team to stay abreast of the evolving information theft-related risks. It would improve sustainable internal control management through effective collaboration of essential IS/IT skills in the ISA team. The collaborative functions between IS auditor and IS/IT encourage two-way communications, which are vital in keeping a spotlight on any potential security risks. It will encourage retail managers to hire and incorporate skilled IS/IT professionals in an ISA team. It will also enhance the management's capacity to counter the trending cases of data leakages and theft resulting from increasing migration of businesses into digital realm.

7.4. INTERDEPENDENCE OF MANAGEMENT IMPROVES INTERNAL INFORMATION THEFT PREVENTION

The interdependence of management in carrying out information security roles improves efficiency in internal information theft prevention. A collaborative relationship between the management and employees is likely to improve employee compliance with IS security policies. The collaborative relationship between cross-functional management (HR, data compliance, IT security, crimes investigation, etc.) is likely to improve the effectiveness of internal data security by directing attention to internal information theft risks and minimizing the challenges encountered by management.

7.4.1 Implication of Interdependence of Management

Internal information theft prevention challenges that have been discussed in Chapter 5 can be minimised by effective management interaction. This key attribute of collaborative security suggests that management interaction can positively impact management performance by minimising the impact of the challenges (e.g., lack of clarity of roles, lack of management support, segregated authority and operational changes). These identified challenges can be a consequence of lack of interaction between management. Management often stick to their roles and practices as they work in their operational environments. If there is no management interaction, conflicts beg the question of which internal information prevention practice to follow. Reconciling these differences and resolving how to act in the face of unfamiliar management often lead to extra work and misunderstanding—and, as a consequentce, extra cost to data security implementation in terms of money, quality and time.

The collaborative sharing of expertise between skilled and experienced management could clarify roles and support issues and impact performance when it comes to implementing data security tools. The complexity of roles in resolving information theft issues in retail operations can be resolved through collaborative role sharing.

The efficiency of effort directed towards prevention of information theft depends on how the roles (security support, information theft incident investigation, data compliance management, security operation, technical security, software engineering, and human resources) interact with each other. The effectiveness of their interaction can be measured by the extent to which they reduce the impact of challenges such as lack of resources, disjointed prevention and data protection policy, IS/T security complexity, lack of clarity of roles, segregated authority, and operational changes.

Lack of effective interaction between management in tackling the challenges can result in lopsided investigation and poor remediation measures. This could have huge implications for the internal security controls and processes employed by retail security management. For instance, there can be implementation of weak internal data control systems and outdated intrusion prevention controls attributed to lax attitudes of management. Steinnon (2006) suggests that some companies fail to identify security risks because the security controls are not working together to keep pace with the evolving technology used by the perpetrators of information theft-related crimes.

7.4.2　Recommendations for Effective Interdependence of Management

An effective collaboration of the audit team would provide better returns on outputs, cost, quality, resources, and time, which neither an independent external audit nor an internal audit would comparatively provide.

With lack of resources, all other roles and responsibilities would be affected. The ripples of this challenge would impact how management learns and reacts to information theft incidents. It would also affect how IS security management implements controls and processes in anticipation of security risks. Lack of resources would have a huge impact on the management without support from internal and external cross-functional management teams—IT security, crime prevention and law enforcement agencies. There is a need for the IS security and crime prevention management roles to be mastered by the cooperative effort of a management team. The mastery roles require effective assurance of the security of the company PII/D assets and, thus, help to implement up-to-date security tools and data compliance regulations to remediate evolving security risks.

For instance, the collaborative ISA approach can enable building of a strong work force across management. The audit team can take control of the internal IS security issues which ease the audit activities, reduce the expended audit time and cut down logistics related to audit protocols. Hooks et al. (1994) suggest that internal information theft risks could be detected and put under control if the organisation and external auditor work together. If the audit team focused more on internal control, they could easily control the organisation's data environment, improve risk assessment and ISA monitoring and enhance the team's communication. Johnson and Rudesill (2012) agree with this suggestion that business owners, management and data security auditors should share the responsibility of internal information theft prevention. There is a need for every unit of the IS management to liaise with each other, prioritise the internal data security and control strategies and be a watchdog for the business. There should be a coordinated approach to assigning the responsibility of IS security. The crack that is often created due to a split in roles of data security can be corrected by effective interrelationship, coordination and communication among the management, external auditing, IT experts and internal auditing.

Engaging in either an independent external audit or an internal audit would require more work on the security auditor's part in carrying out internal control management and audit plans accordingly. However, ISO 19011: 2011 and ACFE (2012) suggested a better chance of external ISA auditors detecting internal information theft risks; such a chance still depends on cooperation of the auditee management. Similarly, engaging in an independent internal audit would do little to meet the expectations of the IS security audit regulatory bodies. An effective exchange of data security strategies between the external and internal auditing should be paramount in companies that are working together to improve their internal data security.

7.4. SUMMARY OF CHAPTER 7

This chapter has provided knowledge, based on case results, of the importance of collaborative management in preventing internal information theft. Adoption of collaborative management in internal information theft prevention has led to redefining the capability of IS security management by examining the workings of collaborative management roles. Although the concept of collaborative security management might not be a universally applicable concept, as there may be some implications in some retail companies, IS security managers can benefit greatly from these insights. For example, as a first step, IS security managers can classify each management role and match it with responsibilities and skills. This could likely produce better role alignment within the IS security management team handling information theft prevention issues. The majority of challenges in the prevention of information theft can be solved through collaborative clarification of different responsibilities to IS security managers. Thus, a collaborative management approach provides a knowledge that can guide information security practitioners to understand and tackle some root causes of other issues on prevention of internal information theft.

However, it may be difficult to assign management with suitable internal information theft prevention roles to make up the management team. These issues might have varying effects across online retail companies, suggesting that some may have utilised collaborative role sharing in their ISA while others did not. As a corollary, it is the role of security and crime prevention management to work with the employees, outsourcing firms and law enforcement agencies. It behooves the management to train cross-functional management and shop-floor employees on how to work collaboratively among themselves while enforcing data security regulations. However, it may not be practicable for retail companies to implement the best data security practices only through trainings, software security, and regulatory strategies.

Proactive strategies such as vulnerability testing on network and web platform, staff vetting and profiling, and customer awareness campaigns might serve as better strategies. Ekblom and Pease (1995) suggest that the applicability of any crime prevention approach, like collaborative security in this guide, would be limited if it is designed without comprehensive contribution of every employee in the organisation. In addition, Ha et al. (2007) argues that software technologies and other technology-based security strategies can foil data breaches, but cannot match the analytic capabilities and creativity of human behaviour, which is paramount in internal information theft prevention. Hence, the next section discusses the theories in the literature that provide an understanding of human behaviour and their application in the context of this guide.

REFERENCES

Association of Certified Fraud Examiners (ACFE), (2012). 'Report to the Nations on Occupational Fraud and Abuse: Global Fraud Study'. Available at: http://www.acfe.com/uploadedFiles/ACFE_Website/Content/rttn/2012-report-to-nations.pdf, Accessed 12/06/2014.

Cilli, C. (2003). 'IT governance: Why a guideline?'. Available: http://m.isaca.org/Journal/Past-Issues/2003/Volume-3/Documents/jpdf033-ITGovernance-Whya-Guideline.pdf, Accessed 23 April 2012.

Ekblom, P. and Pease, K. (1995). 'Evaluating crime prevention'. In: M. Tonry and D.P. Farrington (Eds.), *Building a Safer Society: Strategic Approaches to Crime and Justice. Crime and Justice: A Review of Research, 19.* Chicago: University of Chicago Press, pp. 585–662.

Ha, D., Upadhayaya, S., Ngo, H., Pramanik, S., Chinchani, R. and Mathew, S. (2007). 'Insider threat analysis using information-centric modelling'. *International Federation for Information Processing,* 242(2007), pp. 55–73.

Hooks, K, L. and Kaplan, S, E. and Schultz J, J. (1994). 'Enhancing Communication to Assist in Fraud Prevention and Detection'. *Journal of Practice and Theory,* 13 (2), pp. 86-113.

Innes, M. (2003). *Understanding Social Control: Deviance, Crime and Social Order.* Buckingham: Open University Press.

Johnson, G. G., and Rudesill, C. L. (2001). An investigation into fraud prevention and detection of small businesses in the United States: responsibilities of auditors, managers, and business owners. *Accounting Forum,* 25(1), 56.

McDonald, G. and Nijhof, A. (1999). 'Beyond codes of ethics: An integrated framework for stimulating morally responsible behaviour in organisations'. *Leadership and Organization Development Journal,* 20(3), pp. 133–146.

Nieminski, J. (2008). 'Access and security internal control review'. Internal control review report, 08–3. Audit of HTE and Lenel system access and security, Gresham City.

Okeke, R.I. (2015). 'The prevention of internal identity theft-related crimes: A case study research of the UK online retail companies'. Available: http://ethos.bl.uk/OrderDetails.do?uin=uk.bl.ethos.656978, Accessed 1 August 2015.

Pelletier, K.L. and Bligh, M.C. (2006). 'Rebounding from corruption: Perceptions of ethics programme effectiveness in a public sector organization'. *Journal of Business Ethics*, **67**(4), pp. 359–374.

Potter, C. and Waterfall, G. (2012). 'PriceWaterCoopers' information security breaches survey: Technical report'. Available: www.infosec.co.uk, Accessed 15 October 2012.

Roukis, G.S. (2006). 'Globalisation, organizational opaqueness, and conspiracy'. *Journal of Management Development*, **25**(10), pp. 970–980.

Sekerka, L.E. and Bagozzi, R.P. (2007), 'Moral courage in the workplace: Moving to and from the desire and decision to act'. *Business Ethics: A European Review*, **16**(2), pp. 132–149.

Steinnon, R. (2006). 'Ignoring the insider threat'. *Trade Publication: Network World*, **23**(33), p. 58.

Van Maanen, J. (1974). 'Working the street: "A developmental view of police behaviour"'. In H. Jacob (Ed.), *The Potential for Reform of Criminal Justice. Sage Criminal Justice System Annual Review, 3*. Thousand Oaks, CA: Sage.

8   Application of Criminological Theories to Internal Information Theft Prevention

8.1. INTRODUCTION

Many criminology theorists (e.g., Quinney, 1970; Clarke, 1980; Ekblom, 1992; Cornish, 1994; Aker, 2000; Walker, 2006; Kramer, 2009; Wright, 2010) have studied crime prevention in various research disciplines. As information theft is one of the most prevalent crime issues in business organisations, many theories (e.g., situational prevention, deterrence) have focused on seeking prevention strategies by understanding why people commit these crimes.

This chapter discusses situational crime prevention and deterrence theories that can be applied to the prevention of internal information theft. The theories that have been identified and applied in this chapter are selected because of the attention they have attracted in recent years in academic and security studies.

8.2. CLARKE'S 25 TECHNIQUES OF SITUATIONAL CRIME PREVENTION

Clarke (1980) argues that there is a need to address the factors that create crime 'hotspots' (locations that create crime) and the characteristics that make people more vulnerable to victimisation. In other words, Clarke (1980) suggests that crime prevention measures need to concentrate on preventing crime from occurring and victimisation. These arguments form the basis for Clarke's 25 situational crime prevention techniques. The 25 techniques are built upon the following five main situational crime measures:

1. Increase the effort
2. Increase the risks
3. Reduce the rewards
4. Reduce provocations
5. Remove the excuse

The five key measures that form the basis for Clarke's 25 techniques of situational crime prevention are summarised in Table 8.1 below. Situational crime prevention is underpinned by several theories, including Environmental Criminology, Rational Choice and Routine Activity. The application of these theories and their contribution to prevention of crimes can be extended to the prevention of internal information theft in retail companies. This can be done by adapting Clarke's (1980) 25 techniques of situational crime prevention. The summary of how other measures of situational crime prevention can be extended to the context of prevention of internal information theft in retail companies is provided in Table 8.2 below; instances in the studies of the use of the situational crime prevention measures are discussed.

Target hardening: This measure can be an effective way of reducing opportunities for internal information theft by obstructing employee access by installing anti-copying computer screens applications in call centres and tamper-proof lockers for servers and routers. Ekblom (1992) suggests that the target hardening approach, which was used in the strategy of the anti-bandit screens on post office counters in London in the 1980s, has cut robberies by more than 40 per cent.

Clarke (1999) agrees with Ekblom (1992) and suggests that target hardening was also used in the ticket machines of the London Underground, which has significantly reduced losses related to ticket sales.

Access control: Clarke (1999) suggests that this measure excludes potential offenders from places such as apartments, departments, stores and offices. Cornish and Clarke (1989) suggests that the use of access control in a South London public housing estate and entry phones have significant impact in reducing vandalism and theft. In the context of retail companies, the use of effective personal identification numbers can be implemented to gain access to computer systems, servers, and customers shopping accounts.

Entry/Exit Screening: This is similar to access control but for the purpose of increasing the likelihood of potential criminals being caught if they fail to meet exit/entry requirements. Cornish and Clarke (1989) suggest that this measure has reduced book thefts in the University of Wisconsin library by 80 per cent. In the context of prevention of internal information theft, the use of fob has been introduced in many retail shops and call centres to regulate and monitor staff movements.

These measures could be adapted by retail companies, as summarised in Table 8.2 to reduce the risks of internal information theft. However, several researchers (e.g., Lewis and Sullivan, 1979; Parker, 1998; Clarke, 1999; Willison, 2006) have criticised the extension of the use of situational prevention. Clarke (1999) suggests that the measures may not be 100 per cent effective due to issues such as:

- Technical or administrative ineptitude (Clarke, 1999)
- Measures being defeated by offenders or careless of victims (Cornish and Clarke, 2003)

Table 8.1 Techniques of Situational Crime Prevention (Adapted from Clarke, 1980)

Increase the effort	Increase the risks	Reduce the rewards	Reduce provocations	Remove the excuses
1. **Harden Targets:** Anti-robbery system; quality locks	6. **Extend Guardianship:** Neighbourhood watch	11. **Conceal Targets:** Do not keep valuables in out-of-sight office environment	16. **Reduce frustration and stress:** Efficient queuing; soothing lighting	21. **Set Rules:** Agreements Registration
2. **Control access to facilities:** Secure entries	7. **Assist natural surveillance:** Street lighting; police hotlines	12. **Remove Targets:** Removable car radios; pre-paid phone cards	17. **Avoid Disputes** Reduce crowding in pubs	22. **Post Instructions** 'No parking';'Private property'
3. **Screen Exits** Tickets needed, electronic tags for floor stock	8. **Reduce Anonymity** Taxi driver IDs; 'How's my driving?' signs	13. **Identify Property** Property marking;vehicle licensing	18. **Reduce Emotional Arousal** Control violent Pornography; prohibit paedophiles working with children	23. **Alert Conscience** Roadside speeddisplay signs; 'Shoplifting is stealing'
4. **Deflect Offenders** Street closures in red light district; Separate toilets forwomen	9. **Utilise Place Managers** Train employees to prevent crime; Support whistleblowers	14. **Disrupt Markets** Checks on pawnbrokers; Licensed streetvendors	19. **Neutralise PeerPressure:** Campaigns depicting what friends think of risk-taking behaviour (e.g., speeding and drugcampaigns); "It's ok to say no"	24. **Assist Compliance** Litter bins;Public lavatories
5. **Control Tools/Weapons:** Tougher beer glasses; photos on credit cards	10. **Strengthen Formal Surveillance** Speed cameras; security guards	15. **Deny benefits:** Ink merchandise tags, Graffiti cleaning	20. **Discourage Imitation:** Rapid vandalism repair	25. **ControlDrugs/Alcohol** Breathalysers in pubs, Alcohol-free events

Table 8.2 Adaptation of Situational Crime Prevention Approach for Internal Information Theft

Increase the effort	Increase the risks	Reduce the rewards	Reduce provocation	Remove excuses
1. *Target hardening:*Physical locks for PCs;Anti-copying computer screens in call centres; Tamper-proof lockers for servers and routers	6. *Extend guardianship watch:*Staff watching of visitors; Leave signs of occupancy, Disallow exchange of access privileges	11. *Conceal targets;* Gender-neutral phone directories; Minimise ID access of offices where sensitive information is kept.	16. *Reduce frustrations and stress:* Efficient queues and polite service	21. *Set rules:* Harassment codes; Information security policies
2. *Control access to facilities:*Entry phones; Swipe cards for office access	7. *Assist natural surveillance:* Improved office lighting; Open-plan offices	12. *Remove targets:* Removable data storages; Clear desk and computer screen	17. *Avoid Over rowed office space:* Reduce crowding in call centres	22. *Post instructions:* No pen, paper and pencil.
3. *Screen exits:* Reception desks	8. *Reduce anonymity:*ID tags for staff	13. *Identify property:* Property marking of PCs, laptops and sever systems	18. *Reduce emotional arousal:*Restrict access to how much money is available in customer accounts	23. *Alert conscience:* Create staff awareness to secure computers.
4. *Deflect offenders:*Server and router room closures; Segregation of duties	9. *Utilise place managers:* Two clerks for conveniencestores; Management supervision	14. *Disrupt markets:*Monitor pawn shops	19. *Neutralise peer pressure:* Disperse troublemakers atschool	24. *Assist compliance:* Regulated office checkout and regular holiday for staff; IT security education for staff
5. *Control tools/ weapons:* Disabling stolen cellPhones; Deletion of access rights forex-employees	10. *Strengthen Formalsurveillance:* Security guards; Intrusion detection systems	15. *Deny benefits:* Ink merchandise tags; Encryption	20. *Discourage imitation:* Censor details of modus operandi; Prompt software patching	25. *Control drugs and Alcohol:* Alcohol-free events—end-of-year parties and get-togethers.

- Too much vigilance reduces security consciousness (Clarke and Harris, 1992b)
- Measures may provoke offenders to unacceptable escalation (Hunter and Ray, 1997)
- Some measures facilitate rather than frustrate crimes (Ekblom,1992)
- Lack of proper analysis (user's needs) before introducing some measures (Clarke and Harris, 1992b).
- Detrimental effect of some measures on the environment (Akers, 1990; Willison and Backhouse, 2006).

Collectively, these issues, summarised above, suggest reasons why some situational crime prevention measures like generic and software-based framework (discussed in Chapter 5) may not work in intended ways. This is because measures that work in one setting may not work well in other settings due to organisational and management issues.

Clarke (1999) suggest the need to be aware of these challenges and know which measures work best, in which combination, deployed against what kinds of crimes and under what conditions. Clarke specifically noted that financial costs of particular crime prevention measures need to be assessed by businesses through the development of a permanent in-house capability of their organisations. Hence, there is a need to explore other aspects of crime prevention that may contribute to a holistic approach to internal information theft. The next section discusses deterrence theory and its attributes in internal information theft prevention.

8.3. APPLICATION OF DETERRENCE THEORY TO INFORMATION THEFT PREVENTION

Quinney (1970) suggests that deterrence theory can be traced to the works of classical philosophers (e.g., Thomas Hobbes, Cesare and Beccaria, and Jeremy Bentham). These philosophers provide the foundation for modern deterrence theory in criminology that is classified into two types: general and specific (Aker, 2000). General deterrence, as the name posits, is designed for prevention of crime in the general population, while specific is designed based on the nature of the proscribed sanctions to deter potential crime offenders from committing crimes in the future (Quinney, 1970). Typical instances of the application of the deterrence theory include capital punishment (death penalty) and the use of corporal punishment—Shari 'a/Islamic law in Nigeria, which was introduced in 2001. The deterrence approach to crime prevention deters those who witness the infliction of pains upon the convicted fraudster from committing the crimes themselves (Morgan, 2010). Dobb and Webster (2003) and Wright (2010) argue that punishment as an element of a deterrence theory may be expected to affect the conceptualisation of the deterrence of criminals in two ways.

i. *Increasing the Certainty of Punishment*: This involves deterrence of potential offenders by the risk of apprehension. For instance, if there is increase in the number of security guards monitoring retail call centres, some employees may reduce their dishonest activities in order to avoid being caught.

ii. *Severity of Punishment*: This may influence potential criminal behaviour if potential criminals judge that the consequences of their actions are too severe (Golden, 2002).

Wright (2010) suggests that these elements of punishment underpin the rationale behind 'truth in sentencing policies', to utilise severe sentences to deter some persons from indulging in criminal behaviour.

Some critics (e.g., Willson and Herrnstein, 1985, Moyer, 2001) argue that it is difficult to prove the effectiveness of deterrence because only the offenders that have not been deterred come to the notice of law enforcement. Otherwise, the law enforcement may never know why other employees do not offend. Wright (2010) argues that another reason for deterrence theory's limited application in prevention of crimes *"can be seen by considering the dynamics of the criminal justice system"* (Wright, 2010, p. 3). If there is 100 per cent certainty of apprehending an offender, there would be few potential offenders.

For instance, as cited by Wright (2010), because most crimes (internal information theft, as it is in this guide) do not result in an arrest and conviction because of their complexity, the overall deterrent effect of the certainty of punishment might be substantially reduced. Other critics of deterrence theory (e.g., Williams et al. 1980; Scherdin, 1986; Hirsch et al., 1999; Tonry, 2008) agree that the absence of data on awareness of punishment risks makes it difficult to draw conclusions regarding the deterrent impact of deterrence theory. Hence, it may be difficult to measure the impact of the severity of punishment as a deterrence measure against identity theft related crimes on potential offenders who do not believe they will be apprehended for their dishonest actions.

However, Kramer (2009) argues that deterrence theory can be extended as a traditional security theory and superimposed on the prevention of identity theft related crimes. Haley (2013) agrees with Kramer (2009) and argues that strategic application of deterrence theory in businesses could reduce the costs of cases of internal information theft. Goodman, (2010) argues that many studies of information systems security have not done more to apply tools of deterrence to the prevention of computer crimes. In particular, deterrence theory argues that criminal activities can be eliminated by making costs and consequences outweigh the benefits that may accrue from the criminal acts.

Proponents (e.g., Gibbs, 1968; Quinney, 1970; Akers, 2000) of deterrence theory in the context of employee crimes believe that employees may choose to obey or violate the employee business policy after calculating the consequences and gains of their actions. The uses of the legislation/law enforcement system and digital forensic investigation have proven to be great tools for deterrence of internal information theft in various business sectors.

8.4. LEGISLATIONS/LAW ENFORCEMENT: A DETERRENT TO INTERNAL INFORMATION THEFT

While there may be no silver bullet for effective prevention of internal information theft, the criminal justice system and law enforcement departments can make significant impacts on employees indulging in the crimes (Wright, 2010). Some studies (e.g., Levin, 1971; Orsagh and Chen, 1988; Doob and Webster, 2003; Bavis and Parent, 2007) agree that the criminal justice system increases the *certainty* of punishment, as opposed to the *severity* of punishment, and it is more likely to produce deterrent benefits.

Many countries (e.g., UK, US, Austria, Denmark, France, Germany) across the globe have continued to enact laws and legislation to match the advancement of computer crimes from outside and within business sectors. The common areas of legislation cited in the literature that have been enacted in different countries are as follows:

Privacy Laws and Legislation: This has been used to protect the theft of personal identifiable information of individuals, especially customers of retail companies. Since 1970, the US has used the Fair Credit and Reporting Act and Privacy Act to govern the processing, access, and disclosure of credit information. The same protection of individual privacy was the aim of the Canadian Privacy Act of 1975. The same data privacy protection and governance have been legislated across European countries.

These include the Austrian Federal Data Protection Act of 1978, the Danish Acts on Private Registers, the French Act on Data Processing of 1978, the German Federal Data Protection Act of 1977 and the Swedish Data Act of 1973. Other intellectual property laws have been cited in the literature (e.g., Organisation for Economic Cooperation and Development (OECD), 2013) which have been introduced as a deterrent for the prevention of corporate identity related crimes. These include:

- Intellectual Property and Copyright Law (e.g., Copyright Act of 1976): To deter the theft of trade names, ideas, secrets, computer programmes, personal knowledge, etc. that may be vulnerable to internal identity theft related crimes.
- Trade Secrets Law and Trademark Law: To deter the theft of ideas and trademarks of software and hardware of businesses and organisations.
- Patent Law: To deter theft of software concepts and established products.

To ensure that the deterrence influence of legislation extends to international regions where jurisdictions on privacy laws may differ from the originating venue, the Organisation for Economic Cooperation and Development (OECD) (2013) has introduced the OECD Transborder Data Flow Guidelines to promote effective prevention of internal information theft. The guidelines are designed to prosecute and deter incidents of information theft. For instance, in the US, any employee who is convicted of trafficking or trading passwords or credit cards will be liable to the penalties of Title 18, USC 1029, which include 15 years in prison for the first offence (Identity Theft and Assumption Deterrence Act, 1998). In the UK, violation of Section 55—unlawful obtaining of personal data—makes it an offence for perpetrators of internal identity theft related crimes and hackers outside the organisation to obtain unauthorised access to personal data (Data Protection Act, 1998, Section IV).

8.5. THE USE OF DIGITAL FORENSICS AS INFORMATION THEFT DETERRENCE

Many studies (e.g., Clarke, 1999; Farrington and Petrosino, 2000) agree that an effective use of digital forensics as crime prevention has a deterrence effect on potential perpetrators. Clarke (1999) argues that increasing the perceived risks of committing crimes could deter potential perpetrators. Clarke further explained that this 'situational approach' of crimes prevention can deter an intended or potential criminal, if the criminal knows that there is every certainty of being caught. Farrington and Petrosino (2000) agrees with Clarke (1999) that digital forensic analysis plays a vital role in crimes under investigation, suggesting that fewer crimes would be committed in a business environment where there are such measures.

Drawing on the above suggestion, other studies (Rowlingson, 2005; Walker, 2006; Sommer et al., 2012) have emphasised the importance of digital forensics as a deterrence measure for internal information theft. Rowlingson (2005) suggests that digital forensics can deter potential offenders because of the high risks that the criminal will be caught. If dishonest staffers know that the targeted organisation is policing their corporate IS property with forensic technology, it alerts staffers that their organisation will 'always catch and prosecute thieves'. It may as well act as a psychological deterrent to potential computer related criminals (Gottfredson and Taylor, 1986; Walker, 2006).

Moreover, digital forensic investigation practice may encourage and intensify the mindset of natural surveillance to potential information theft perpetrators (Sommer et al., 2012). It provides demonstrative evidence during the courtroom prosecution of suspects. Welch (1997) argues that evidence generated through digital forensic investigation convinces the jury beyond a reasonable doubt that the offender is guilty of the offence.

Bhati (2010) suggests that there is no doubt that digital forensic evidence greatly deters criminal behaviour. In his study '*Quantifying the Specific Deterrent Effects of DNA Databases*', Bhati (2010) tested the specific deterrent effect of digital forensic DNA evidence on crimes. He concluded that deterrence of digital evidence has probative effect ranges from 20 per cent to 30 per cent. Taylor et al. (2007) agree with Bhati (2010) in their deterrence theory and suggest that digital forensic evidence could be used as a deterrence measure to prevent internal information theft.

8.6. SUMMARY OF CHAPTER 8

As the discussion of crime prevention theories in this chapter shows, situational crime prevention theories, the deterrent effect of the criminal justice system and digital forensic investigations may substantially reduce incidents of internal information theft. However, the impact of the deterrent on the prevention of internal information theft may be dependent on the extent of awareness that potential offenders have in relation to the deterrence measures. Based on the existing evidence presented here, there is a need for both security management and crime prevention management to apply deterrence theories along with other security practices to ensure the likelihood of detecting criminal behaviour. Chapter 10 will discuss recommended security practices that can be used to supplement crime prevention theories to achieve effective information theft prevention in retail businesses.

REFERENCES

Akers, R.L. (1990). 'Rational choice, deterrence, and social learning theory in criminology: The path not taken'. *Journal of Criminal Law and Criminology*, 81(3), pp. 654–656.
Akers, R.L. (2000). *Criminological Theories*. Los Angeles: Roxbury.
Bavis, C. and Parent, M. (2007). 'Data theft or loss: ten things your lawyer must tell you about handling information'. *Ivey Business Journal Online*, 76(6), pp. 1–9.
Bhati, A. (2010). *Quantifying the Specific Deterrent Effects of DNA Databases*. Washington, DC: Justice Policy Centre; The Urban Institute, pp. 1–59.
Clarke, R.V. (1980). 'Situational crime prevention: Theory and practice'. *British Journal of Criminology*, 20, pp. 136–147.
Clarke, R.V. (1999). *Hot Products: Understanding, Anticipating and Reducing the Demand for Stolen Goods, Police Research Series, 98*. London: Home Office.
Clarke, R.V. and Harris, P. (1992) 'A rational choice perspective on the target of auto theft'. *Criminal Behaviour and Mental Health*, 2, pp. 25–42.
Cornish, D. (1994). 'The procedural analysis of offending and its relevance for situational prevention'. In: R. Clarke (Ed.), *Crime Prevention Studies*. New York: Criminal Justice Press, pp. 151–196.
Cornish, D. and Clarke, R.V. (1989). 'Crime specialisation, crime displacement and rational choice theory'. In: H. Wegener, F. Losel and J. Haisch (Eds.), *Criminal Behaviour and the Justice System: Psychological Perspective*. New York: Springer-Verlag, pp. 103–117.
Cornish, D.B. and Clarke, R.V. (2003). 'Opportunities, precipitators and criminal decisions: A reply to Wortley's critique of situational crime prevention'. *Crime Prevention Studies*, 16(2003), pp. 41–96.

Dobb, A. and Webster, C. (2003). 'Sentence severity and crime: Accepting the null hypotheses'. *Crime and Justice*, 30, pp. 143–195.

Ekblom, P. (1992). 'Preventing post office robberies in London: Effects and side effects'. In: R.V. Clarke (Ed.), *Situational Crime Prevention: Successful Case Studies*. Albany, NY: Harrow and Heston, pp. 36–43.

Farrington, D.P. and Petrosino, A. (2000). 'Systematic reviews of criminological interventions: The Campbell Collaboration Crime and Justice Group'. *International Annals of Criminology*, 38(2001), pp. 49–66.

Gibbs, J.P. (1968). 'Crime, punishment and deterrence. South-western'. *Social Science Quarterly*, 48, pp. 515–530.

Golden, L. (2002). *Evaluation of the Efficacy of a Cognitive Behavioural Program for Offenders on Probation: Thinking for a Change*. Dallas: University of Texas.

Goodman, W. (2010). 'Cyber deterrence: Tougher in theory than in practice'. *Strategic Studies Quarterly*, 4(3), p. 103

Gottfredson, S. and Taylor, R.B. (1986). 'Environmental design, crime and prevention: An examination of community dynamics'. In: M. Tory and A.J. Reiss (Eds.), *Communities and Crime*. Chicago: University of Chicago Press, pp. 387–416.

Haley, C. (2013). 'A theory of cyber deterrence'. *Georgetown Journal of International Affairs*, Available: http://Journal.Georgetown.Edu/A-Theory-Of-Cyber-Deterrence-Christopher-Haley, Accessed 23 April 2014.

Hirsch, A. Bottoms, A., Burney, E. and Wikstrom, P.O. (1999). *Criminal Deterrence and Sentence Severity: An Analysis of Recent Research*. Oxford: Hart Publishing.

Hunter, R. and Ray, J.C. (1997). Preventing convenience store robbery through environmental design. In: R. Clarke (Ed.), *Situational Crime Prevention: Successful Case Studies* (2nd edn.). New York: Harrow and Heston, pp. 146–192.

Kramer, F.D. (2009). 'Policy recommendations for a strategic framework'. In: F.D. Kramer, H.S. Stuart and L.K. Wentz (Eds.), *Cyberpower and National Security*. Dulles: National Defence University Press and Potomac Books, Inc., p. 15.

Levin, M.A. (1971). 'Policy Evaluation and Recidivism'. *Law and Society Review*, 6(1), pp. 17–46.

Lewis, E.R. and Sullivan, T.T. (1979). 'Combating crime and citizen attitudes: A study of the corresponding reality'. *Journal of Criminal Justice*, 7, pp. 71–79.

Morgan, P.M. (2010). 'Applicability of traditional deterrence concepts and theory to the cyber realm', Paper presented at a workshop on deterring cyber-attacks, Washington, DC, p. 57.

Moyer, I.L. (2001). *Criminological Theory: Traditional and Non-Traditional Voices and Themes*. Thousand Oaks, CA: Sage.

Organisation for Economic Cooperation and Development (OECD). (2013). 'OECD guidelines governing the protection of privacy and trans-border flows of personal data'. Available: http://www.oecd.org/sti/ieconomy/2013-oecd-privacy-guidelines.pdf, Accessed 30 November 2013.

Orsagh, T. and Chen, J.R. (1988). 'The effect of time served on recidivism: An interdisciplinary theory'. *Journal of Quantitative Criminology*, 4(2), pp. 155–171.

Parker, D. (1998). *Fighting Computer Crime: A New Framework for Protecting Information*. New York: Wiley Computer Publishing.

Quinney, R. (1970). *The Social Reality of Crime*. Boston: Little, Brown.

Rowlingson, R. (2005). 'An introduction to forensic readiness planning'. Centre for the Protection of National Infrastructure (CPNI) technical note, pp. 1–13.

Scherdin, M.J. (1986). 'The halo effect: psychological deterrence of electronic security systems'. *Information Technology and Libraries*, 5(3), pp. 232–235.

Sommer, P. (3rd edn.). (2012). 'Digital Evidence, Digital Investigations and E-Disclosure: A Guide to Forensic Readiness for Organisations, Security Advisers and Lawyers'. Information AssuranceAdvisory Council, UK.

Taylor, R.B., Goldkamp, J.S., Weiland, D., Breen, C., Garcia, R.M., Presley, L.A. and Wyant, B.R. (2007). 'Revise policies mandating offender DNA collection'. *Criminology and Public Policy*, 6(4), pp. 851–862.

Tonry, M. (2008). 'Learning from the limitations of deterrence research'. In: M. Tonry (Ed.), *Crime and Justice: A Review of Research*. Chicago: The University of Chicago Press, pp. 279–306.

Walker, C. (2006). 'Computer forensics: Bringing the evidence to court'. Available: http://www.infosecwriters.com/text_resources/pdf/Computer_Forensics_to_Court.pdf, Accessed 24 January 2013.

Welch, T. (1997). 'Computer crime investigation and computer forensics'. *Information systems security*, 6(2), pp. 25–56.

Williams, K.R., Gibbs, J.P. and Erickson, M.L. (1980). 'Public knowledge of statutory penalties: The extent and basis of accurate perception'. *Pacific Sociological Review*, 23(1), pp. 105–128.

Willison, R. (2006). 'Understanding the perpetration of employee computer crime in the organisational context'. *Information and Organisation*, 16(4), pp. 304–324.

Willison, R. and Backhouse, J. (2006). 'Opportunities for computer crime: Considering systems risk from a criminological perspective'. *European Journal of Information Systems*, 15(4), pp. 403–414.

Willson, J.Q. and Herrnstein, R.J. (1985). *Crime and Human Nature*. New York: Simon and Schuster.

Wright, V. (2010). 'Deterrence in Criminal Justice Evaluating Certainty vs. Severity of Punishment'. *The Sentencing Project Research and Advocacy for Reform*, pp.1–9.

9 Recommended Practices for Internal Information Theft Prevention

9.1 INTRODUCTION

This chapter discusses recommended security practices garnered from renowned IS security consulting firms and research experts. Information security strategies are practices that ensure that employees do not steal and leak sensitive/critical retail business information. The strategies include software products that can help security professionals control what information employees can process during retail operation.

Although adoption of rigorous security strategies is very important, the effectiveness of strategies in preventing internal information theft depends on these practices: security of employees, implementing internal proprietary security/control, well-defined corporate policies and information security audits. This chapter helps the reader to understand the importance of these practices in the prevention of internal information theft through an in-depth analysis of multiple case studies, reports and recommendations.

9.2 SECURITY PRACTICES FOR INTERNAL INFORMATION THEFT PREVENTION

Vulnerabilities and Patch Management are among the top five security strategies recommended for the prevention of internal information theft. Retail companies should ensure that vulnerability and patch management of security software are maintained and updated. This suggests that vulnerabilities management is an essential data security tool and that maintenance should be the core statistic of a security metric for any business IS security. Along with vulnerability management, code and configuration reviews were suggested as elements that need to be given priority in patch and vulnerability management.

Other security strategies that are suggested by the firms are Application and Data Security, threat identification focused on Internal Human Threats, Controlled Access Based on the Need to Know and User Security Training and Awareness. In particular, User Security Training and Awareness, threat identification focused on Internal Human Threats and Controlled Access Based on the Need to Know were also given a high level of priority, as these are directly related to end-user and human roles in retail businesses.

Microsoft's Enhanced Mitigation Experience Toolkit (EMET) suggests that IS managers should focus on finding specific internal information theft vulnerabilities, and it blocks potential security exploits (TechNet Blogs, 2013). SANS Critical Security Controls, (2008) suggests that conventional information theft prevention based on data security certainly has its place, although the success of the prevention strategies depends mostly on how the IS security management implements them.

Other suggestions, like the Kill-chain approach (KCA) suggested by Lockheed and Hutchin (2010), essentially recommend the integration of both technology and human roles in mitigation approaches, with much emphasis on the process of implementation as the key linked to KCA success.

Table 9.1 summarises the internal information prevention strategies according to the priority that should be given in implementing them. This priority is suggested by case reports by the Forrester Seeburger (2013). They are arranged in decreasing order of the priority that they should be given by companies.

Other strategies recommended by Forrester Seeburger Security and the Consortium for Cyber Security Action include: complementing the business security required with business partners/third parties; integrating physical and logical security; e-Discovery; engaging law enforcement agencies; security outsourcing; complying with security requirements placed upon businesses by their partners; limitations and control of network ports, protocols, and services; controlled use of administrative privileges; boundary defence; maintenance, monitoring, and analysis of security audit; Controlled Access Based on the Need to Know; account monitoring and control; data loss prevention; incident response and management, and secure network engineering

9.3 PRACTICES FOR INTERNAL INFORMATION THEFT PREVENTION

Information process risk assessment and training of employees to recognise bogus information processing and applications (credit card, bank account) have proven to be one of the top security strategies in preventing information theft. Most security consultants agree that retail companies that adhere to the practices of effective data protection and compliance management often succeed in preventing information theft. The UK Data Protection Act of 1984 and 1998 and the Information Commissioner's Office provide the guidelines for internal information theft prevention through effective protection of customer data, a thorough employee recruitment process, and secure record management, effective monitoring of employees, and structured training of employees on information theft awareness. However, it

Table 9.1 Recommended Practices for Information Theft Prevention

Priority	Forrester Seeburger Security	Consortium for Cyber security Action	Global Information Assurance and Data Security Essentials
1	Data Security	Inventory of Authorised and Unauthorised Devices	System Characterisation and defining the scope and boundaries IS
2	Managing vulnerability and threats	Inventory of Authorised and Unauthorised Software	Threat Identification focused on Internal Human Threats
3	Business continuity/ disaster recovery	Secure Configurations for Hardware and Software on Laptops, Workstations, and Servers	Vulnerability Identification in Information Systems
4	Managing information risk	Continuous Vulnerability Assessment and Remediation	Control Analysis and Review of Data Security Controls
5	Application security	Malware Defences	Likelihood Determination of possible Exploit/ Vulnerability
6	Aligning IT security with the business	Application software security	Impact analysis
7	Regulatory compliance	Wireless Device Control	Risk determination of exposure to information theft (low, medium, high)
8	Cutting costs and /or increasing efficiency	Data Recovery Capability	Results, documentation and process presentation
9	Identity and access management	Security skills assessment and appropriate training to fill gaps	Data security control recommendations
10	User security training and awareness	Secure configurations for network devices such as firewalls, routers, and switches	Penetration Test

is important to note that the success of these guidelines is reliant on the readiness of retail management to effectively implement them. The following sections summarise information theft prevention practices, although not the exhaustive lists of the practices.

9.3.1 Security of Critical Retail Business Assets

The security of critical retail business assets, partly discussed in Chapter 2, is very important. The effective security of the key business assets—people and property—can immensely enhance effective prevention of internal information theft in retail businesses.

People: Security of Employees

Awareness of mechanisms for stealing information within retail business creates a sense of confidence in the employees and equips them with knowledge to prevent information theft risks. The UK Credit Industry Fraud Avoidance System (CIFAS) has suggested that employee awareness of collusion, coercion and collaboration is one of the most effective prevention practices for information theft.

In addition, good reporting procedures for information theft cases/incidents rebuild employee confidence that such cases would be handled according to the business ethics of their organisations. Three major practices have been commonly adopted by businesses to complement the security of employees: vetting and screening of employees, staff monitoring, and staff profiling.

Vetting and Screening of Employees: Background screening of current or potential employees is a first line of security in the prevention of internal information theft. Effective screening can reduce the risks associated with retail businesses employing potentially dishonest employees. CIFAS's *'Enemy Within'* suggests that lack of checks and controls during recruitment increases the risks of employing dishonest employees that may pose internal information theft risks. Thorough recruitments checks and controls do not only identify the dishonest staff prone to committing internal information theft and related fraud but also prevent the infiltration of the employees alike. These findings suggest the need for the relentless effort of personnel managers in vetting processes in many retail companies. If the fight against internal information theft related crimes is ever going to succeed, prospective employers must ensure the credible vetting of all new employees.

Staff Monitoring: This is monitoring of employees through human resources (HR) and promotion of the internal corporate culture of employees. Companies with a good tradition of internal HR management have fewer cases of internal information theft compared to those without. Businesses invest a lot of resources to secure their IS infrastructure from external attack sources like hackers but neglect the threat posed by dishonest employees. HR management can promote effective monitoring of the employees who are living a suspicious lifestyle that may pose potential threats to the business.

HR managers can create a desirable culture in every organisation by promoting: fraud management policy, employee fraud prevention policy, code of conduct or business ethics, disciplinary policy, fraud reporting policy, whistleblowing policy, staff assistance policy and fraud specialist policy. It is important for businesses to set standards of employees' information processing culture/conducts, which should be monitored, and effectively guided by the information protection policies. Although legal action against dishonest employees and fraudsters based on the business policy might be expensive, it still serves as deterrence for potential perpetrators and their collaborators.

Case Study 9.1   Information Theft Risks Associated with Recruitment

UK Fraud Advisory Panel (2011) reports that the majority of potential employees lie in their job applications. In their report, it was indicated that 25 per cent of the curriculum vitae of the applicants examined were falsified with information related to academic qualifications and employment histories to secure their potential employment. This report also recorded that 34 per cent of managers failed to check the background of their prospective employees. Of all companies that were surveyed by the Chartered Institute of Personnel Development (CIPD) cited in Hinds (2007), only 77 per cent of the companies cross-check their potential candidate references. One may argue that the remaining 23 per cent is smaller compared to the 77 per cent, but this could do much more damage to any organisation, considering the impact of internal information theft.

Staff Profiling: This is a technique of developing a behavioural pattern of an information theft suspect. Profiling can encourage effective risk analysis and paves the way for thorough investigation, and the outcome can be used as a guide for changing information security strategies and amending policies within organisations. Profiling helps businesses to establish which job roles or business areas pose the most information theft risks and enables the intelligence services to design predictive modelling tools.

9.3.2. Security of Proprietary Information Systems

Retail companies should invest more on security systems and controls to avoid being targeted as the weakest link. The advancement of the information technology has enabled information theft perpetrators to continue to refine and update their techniques. For instance, the recent 2011 Sony PlayStation Network (PSN) attack remained a lesson for the business organisation that thorough and updated proprietary information security is indispensable for internal information security. If PSN was thoroughly subjected to internal data and proprietary security and other rigorous intrusion detection control tests, perhaps, the compromise of the about 70 million users' personal identifiable information would have been averted. Although there is still evidence that the cause of the PSN attack was linked to a dishonest act within the company, the need for effective internal data proprietary security monitoring remains obvious. Cases of internal information theft, as presented in Case Study 9.2, are still rampant because of the security loopholes of the IT infrastructures and proprietary systems. However, some of the new complex technologies that have been noted to have proven security for process, property and proprietary information security are biometric technologies, cryptography, authentication and certification and single-sign on technologies.

Although some of these leading data security technology solutions—IBM AppScan, forensic data warehousing, Vontu by Symantec—exist, companies might not make much out these security tools if there is no effective security audit and compliance management.

Case Study 9.2   Risks Associated with Proprietary Information Systems

Dean (2012) reported in Ponemon Institute Research that 28 per cent of the internal information theft cases in 583 US companies occurred among the mobile workforce, of which 44 per cent of the companies surveyed still view their IT infrastructure as relatively insecure, while 90 per cent have had cases of information theft at least once in the prior 12 months. This report shows that some business organisations, including retail companies, allow their employees to store valuable customer personal identifiable information on online applications such as Google Docs and Dropbox.

Verizon DBIR (2012) agrees with Dean (2012) and indicates that out of 447 business organisations that participated in their survey of how employers use social media in their business, 52 per cent of small businesses depend on social networking sites, with only 8 per cent of small businesses monitoring what staff post on those sites. These business practices expose the data to theft and make customer PID/I vulnerable to information theft. In some cases, the use of social networking sites—LinkedIn, Twitter, Facebook—leaves digital trails that make online companies susceptible to social engineering.

9.4 THE STRATEGY FOR INFORMATION THEFT PREVENTION

This strategy was developed to support federal, state and local law enforcement agencies for the prevention of internal information theft and has been recommended for adoption in US businesses. The seven main components of US national strategy are information protection, legislation, partnerships and collaboration, public awareness, reporting procedures, training, and victim assistance. It is vital to emphasise the three key components—legislation, partnership and collaboration and training—because they extend the understanding of the prevention strategies that have been discussed in section 9.2.1 and because of the suggested impacts these practices can have on internal information theft prevention. Table 9.1 summarises these three components.

Table 9.2   Strategy for Internal Information Theft Prevention

Strategy	Features and impact on information theft prevention
Partnership and Collaboration	Strategy for effective information theft prevention has been adopted in many business organisations in the following instances: Indiana State Police for the US Strategic Alliances, Computer and IT and National White Collar Crime Centre (NW3C), 'Tiered Approach' among students and IS/T security experts, Scientific Working Group on Digital Evidence (SWDGE), the Nigeria's Police Economic and Financial Crimes Commission ("EFCC"), the UK's Central Sponsor of Information Assurance and Office of Cyber Security Office and Cyber Security and Information Assurance (OSCIA), the UK's anti-fraud scheme—TRADE (Transactis Risk Assessment Data Exchange) which shares transactional data to enable the detection of potential information theft and computer related criminals and fraudsters in business organisations, the Defence Advanced Research Projects Agency (DARPA). These collaborative bodies work with an aim to establish standard practices to guide professionals in investigating identity theft crimes and other computer related crimes. They work together, sharing their expertise, both in areas of provision of digital investigatory strategies and evidence, to foster the security threats of businesses. Rosenberg (2010) suggests that a partnership approach, which is used in biological and nuclear arm controls treaties, could help prevent identity theft crimes and encourage robust practices in investigating these crimes across nations, business organisations, industries and sectors.

(*Continued*)

Table 9.2   (Continued)

Strategy	Features and impact on information theft prevention
Legislation	The harmonisation of data privacy and security legislation across businesses can reduce the bottlenecks during information theft case reporting. Bringing together various cross-border data protection policies provides the opportunity for thorough investigation of information theft in the emerging business networking and outsourcing. This harmonised policy approach to preventing internal information theft at an international level is an indispensable practice that has been pioneered by US governments. Comprehensive legislation on information theft prevention can help to tackle the challenges related to 'the admissibility' of electronic evidence and other related legal hurdles. Breyer (2012) suggests in the Reference Manual on Scientific Evidence that law seeks decisions that fall within the boundaries of scientifically sound knowledge, but it is sometimes difficult to achieve in practice if there is no existing policy on crimes prevention to support provision for the scientific evidence.
Training	Continuous training for retail staffers can help immensely to match the evolution of the Information Systems application in retail operations. An anonymous New Jersey Regional Computer Forensics Laboratory (NJRCFL) director and FBI supervisory special agent noted the importance of staff training. He said that being an IT/S security expert in preventing information theft is '*not only what I know, but what I know that is not so*'. It is now the responsibility of computer security experts to update their skills and knowledge of information theft prevention.The G8 on standards for the Exchange of Digital Evidence also emphasised the need for training security experts in preventing information theft. Their argument is based on the conventional security certification: because there are certifications for fraud investigators in other fields (accounting, finance, and banking), the need for certified professional examinations for information theft in computer crimes should be given due consideration.

9.5 PRACTICE OF INFORMATION SYSTEMS GOVERNANCE AND SECURITY INTELLIGENCE

Global Information Assurance Certification (GIAC) recommends that practices including IS/T monitoring and CCTV and network intrusion detection systems, system characterisation, and information theft incidents results documentations can improve detection of the likelihood that a privileged user or a dishonest employee may exploit a known vulnerability.

In addition, GIAC claims that application of the control analyses reduces the risks of insider threats to system vulnerability and that control tools such as DirectoryAlert and ServerAlert by NetVision can reduce potential information theft risks.

Forrester and Seeburger (2013) agree with Conte (2003) and suggest three key elements—Define Your Data, Dissect Your Data, and Defend Your Data—for effective internal data security intelligence against internal information theft. Dissection of the data is the process of critical data analytics for security intelligence. It can be defined with an acronym: INTEL—Information, Notification, Threats, Evaluation and Leadership. With efficient data definition and data dissection in place, these principles would enhance the security of information processing in retail businesses.

In addition, efficient implementation of these practical elements could reduce data leakages by encouraging the principle of least privilege—strictly enforce access control, inspect data usage patterns to identify abuse, dispose of data when no longer needed and encrypt data to limit the access. Forrester and Seeburger (2013) further suggest that data with defined location and index would facilitate the development of a life cycle for data classification, cataloguing and data discovery to reduce information theft risks.

9.6 THE USE OF THE INFORMATION SECURITY AUDIT (ISA)

It is important that retail businesses utilise the above prevention strategies—proprietary security, with IS security audit playing the critical role in implementing those strategies. The Association of Certified Fraud Examiners (ACFE) suggested that an effective information security audit is more likely to unveil security loopholes and prevent internal information theft risks.

Since an information security audit plays a substantial role in the security of information processing in retail operations, as discussed in Chapter 7, security managers must make a substantial investment in ISA to protect consumers' PII/D from the emerging social and technological oriented information theft risks. It could be argued that half the combined cost of internal information theft could be the cost of their prevention through effective ISA. Hence, businesses should prioritise practical and strategic IS security checks to avert data leakages which originate from inside business organisations. Case Study 9.3 summarises the investment efforts of UK and US business organisations, as shown by Pricewatercoopers and ACFE surveys.

Case Study 9.3   Impact of Security Audit on Information Theft Prevention

The PWC's information security breaches (ISB) (2014) reports that 50 per cent of UK companies plan to spend more on IT security and that there was an increase of 9 per cent in 2012 over the previous year. This report also indicated that the UK Cyber Security Operations Centre spends more than £5 million annually on information security issues, while the US federal agencies budgeted about $6.5 billion on data security assurance alone for the fiscal year 2012.

PWC's Report (2014) on the strategies for identifying information theft risks in business organisations noted that ISA was rated at 75 per cent while other strategies such as IS breakdown and loss of company assets account for 25 per cent. In addition, ACFE (2014) suggested that more than 43 per cent of information theft cases were detected by use of the ISA, of which 7 per cent were detected by independent external security auditing. This report shows that more than 50 per cent of such crimes could be detected by an effective Information Systems security audit.

9.7 INTERNAL INFORMATION DETECTION MECHANISMS AS PREVENTION PRACTICE

Use of internal information theft detection mechanisms available to retail businesses would guide the understanding of some elements required for designing effective preventive strategies. It would enable the businesses to make decisions on resource allocation and the implementation know-how on when and how to apply them. Top research organisations (e.g., ISACA, British Retail Consortium (BRC) and Verizon's Data Breach Investigation Report (DBIR) claimed that detecting internal information theft at the earliest stages of escalation results in fewer repercussions, although not fewer than if these incidents were prevented. This claim suggests that use of the IS/T security controls may not offer absolute detection mechanism as they have their downsides—cost, complexity and implementation. However, attention should be directed towards understanding the timeline of internal information theft incidents in relation to detection. Understanding the time frame for incidents could increase the ability to provide comprehensive prevention capability evaluation. The time span or timeline for internal information theft incidents depends on a variety of factors and incident detection processes.

The Verizon's DBIR (2014) categorised the timeline analysis of information theft incidents into three phases: pre-incident, active incident and post-incident. The pre-incident phase is the initial phase of the incident which depicts time from the first action taken against the victimised company by the perpetrator until the time when IS/T property is affected. This is common with network resources intrusions and point of sale (POS) abetted hacks. According to Verizon's (2013) DBIR Report, 85 per cent of internal information theft incidents under this phase occurred within minutes or less. The time for the pre-incident phase depends on the complexity of security platform of the victim companies. BRC indicates that large retail companies have a shorter pre-incident time than smaller companies because of the complexities associated with managing large IS/T infrastructure and detecting crimes in large retail companies.

The active-incident phase covers the timespan from the pre-incident phase to the time when PID/I is first removed from the victims' IS/T control environment. In average, the time for this incident phase is longer—the time it takes the perpetrator to explore the network, locate and exploit the relevant IS/T platforms and then exfiltrate/collect the critical information. Figure 9.1 (adapted from Verizon's DBIR, 2013) summarises the approximate days taken for internal information theft incident to be detected by various mechanisms: actor disclosure, fraud detection, monitoring service, law enforcement, audit, anti-virus, etc.

Case Study 9.4   Information Theft Detection Mechanisms and Time Span

The Computer Security Incident Handling Guide (Chichonski et al., 2012, see Figure 9.1) shows that it takes 15 months for the fraud detection team and nine months for the law enforcement, compared to less than six months recorded for the same incidents to be detected by the internal party. There could be various reasons attributed to these delays in detecting internal information theft cases. In some cases, the nature of the business operation may lead to delays; the victim companies might have contingency plans in place to manage the business disruption while the investigation can be carried out. Another reason attributed to the delays associated with detecting the internal information theft incidents is that more than 78 per cent of the incidents are committed during working hours. In some cases when the incident were not committed during the working hours, more than 50 percent of internal information theft cases were detected months after the departure of the perpetrators from the victimised companies.

The Computer Security Incident Handling Guide (CSIHG) posits that abetted SQL injection related incidents fall into the active-incident phase and are common in both small and bigger retail companies. The post-incident phase describes the time from the active-incident phase to the time the victim discovers the incident. Some internal information theft cases which are categorised as post-incident could remain undiscovered for months. The post-incident phase may cover as much as months. Some cases can take years because the perpetrators cover their trails, especially in the case of incidents that are perpetrated by software engineer/administrators. This phase could extend to as much time as it takes the victim to detect or to

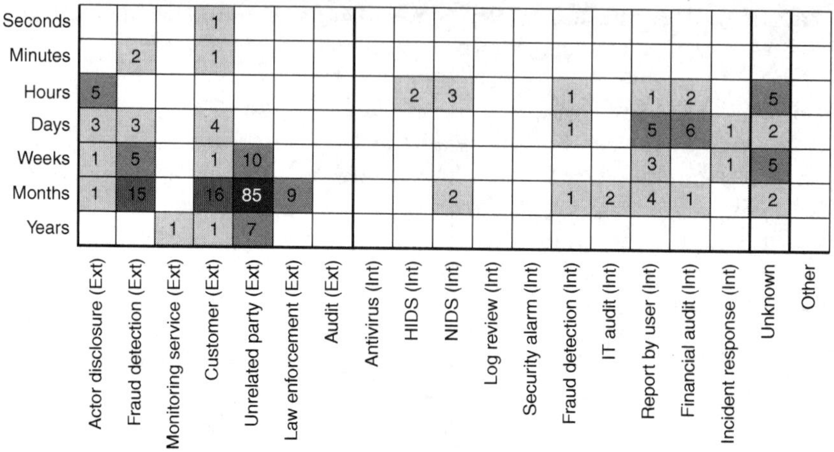

	Actor disclosure (Ext)	Fraud detection (Ext)	Monitoring service (Ext)	Customer (Ext)	Unrelated party (Ext)	Law enforcement (Ext)	Audit (Ext)	Antivirus (Int)	HIDS (Int)	NIDS (Int)	Log review (Int)	Security alarm (Int)	Fraud detection (Int)	IT audit (Int)	Report by user (Int)	Financial audit (Int)	Incident response (Int)	Unknown	Other
Seconds			1																
Minutes		2	1																
Hours	5								2	3				1	1	2		5	
Days	3	3	4										1		5	6	1	2	
Weeks	1	5	1	10											3		1	5	
Months	1	15	16	85	9							2		1	2	4	1	2	
Years			1	1	7														

Figure 9.1   Information Theft Detection Mechanisms (Time Span) (Chichonski et al., 2012)

discover the security breach, which sometimes proves impossible. Most post-incident cases are discovered by external parties (e.g., notification by an informant/customer, law enforcement, competing organisations, Internet Service Providers).

Case Study 9.5   Detection of Internal Information Theft in Small and Large Businesses

Verizon's DBIR (2012, 2013) suggests that more than 50 per cent of internal information theft cases in large business organisation were detected by an external party, whereas, in aggregate, irrespective of the size, 92 per cent of these known incidents were detected by the same external party (see Figure 9.2). The larger companies recorded only 16 per cent of the active detection by an internal party and only 2 per cent of internal detection was recorded in all the organisations studied. But, in all, external parties are the largest source of internal information incident detection. In particular, Verizon DBIR (2013), as shown in Figure 9.3, suggests that few technical methods could be used to detect information theft incidents. The reports agrees that end-user activities are the most effective means of detecting information theft incidents. End-users can detect information theft through suspicious e-mails and slow system performance in the course of their daily job operations. Other common internal methods include fraud financial audit, log review, IT audit, and incident response (see Figure 9.3).

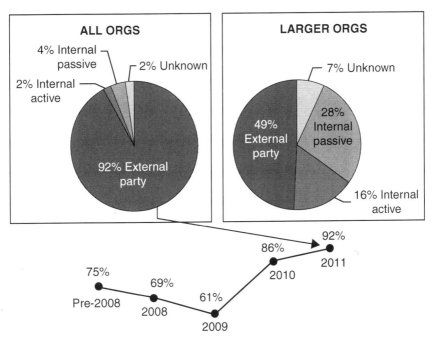

Figure 9.2 Detection of Internal Information Theft in Small/Large Org. (Verizon DBIR, 2012)

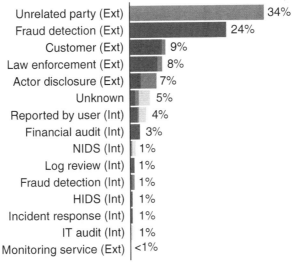

Figure 9.3 Detection Mechanisms for Internal Information Theft (Verizon's DBIR, 2013)

9.8 SUMMARY OF CHAPTER 9

As a summary to this chapter, Table 9.3 lists common methods of perpetrating internal information theft in retail businesses and the corresponding recommended prevention and detection strategies. However, it is important to emphasise that retail companies should implement the recommendations which might be practicable in relation to their size and business processes. Even with the most recommended prevention practices that have been recognised and implemented by a consortium of security professionals, there is no *one-size-fits-all* internal information prevention or detection strategy/ practice. Hence, the application and implementation of practices and strategies across business operations will differ depending on budget, business need, and process and size.

Table 9.3   Perpetration of Internal Information Theft and Respective Detection and Prevention

Mechanisms	Detection	Prevention
Infiltrated hacking: access to protect IS with stolen credential.	Monitoring of administrative/privilege activity: logon time, anomalies, malware on the system	Controlled authentication: two faction, Internet protocol blacklisting, internal restricted administrative connection.
Abetted botnet and infiltration.	Registry monitoring and examination of the active system processes.	Integrity control mechanisms, Egress filtering via ports and protocols, host intrusion detection systems (IDS), updating firewalls and software security.
Tampering and copying of PID/I	Some scratches on the IS device, Bluetooth signals.	Employees training, Consistent inspection, policy implementation, anti-tampering tools—tamper switch, epoxy electronics.
Social engineering and manipulation	Call logs, e-mail logs, unusual communication, bypass of technological alerting mechanisms, visitors' log.	Clearly defined policies and procedures, general security awareness training.
Collusion and employees abetted cybercrimes	Routine monitoring of the databases, webserver, IDS and intrusion prevention systems (IPS)	Principles of least privilege account management, input validation and whitelisting techniques

(Continued)

Table 9.3   (Continued)

Mechanisms	Detection	Prevention
Collaboration with external agents	Last logon banner, end-user behavioural analysis, logon source location analysis	Disabling default account, scanning of passwords, password-change rotation principle, sharing of the administrative duties.
SQL via back-end databases	Desk calls for account lockouts, sequential guessing and log in attempts failures.	Password policy, password throttling and effective access control mechanisms.

REFERENCES

Association of Certified Fraud Examiners (ACFE). (2014). 'Report to the nations on occupational fraud and abuse: global fraud study'. Available: http://www.acfe.com/rttn/docs/2014-report-to-nations.pdf, Accessed 20 April 2014.

Breyer, S. (2012). *Reference Manual on Scientific Evidence* (3rd edn). Washington, DC: The National Academies Press, pp. 1–968.

Cichonski, P., Millar, T., Grance, T. and Scarfone, K. (2012). 'Computer security incident handling guide', SP 800–61, Revision. NIST. Available: http://csrc.nist.gov/publications/nistpubs/800–61 rev2/SP800–61 rev2.pdf, Accessed 27 October 2012.

Conte, J.M. (2003). 'Cyber security: Looking inward internal threat evaluation'. Global Information Assurance Certification (GIAC) Security Essentials Certification (GSEC) paper, practical assignment version 1.4b, pp. 1–13.

Dean et al., (2011). Cost of Data Breach Study: Global, Ponemon Institute Research Report, Available: http://www.ponemon.org/local/upload/file/2011_US_CODB_FINAL_5.pdf, Accessed 23/03/2014.

Dean, S., Pett, J., Holcomb, C., Roath, D. and Sharma, N. (2012). 'Fortifying your defences: The role of internal audit in assuring data security and privacy'. PCW Publications. Available: http://www.PWC.com/us/en/risk-assurance-services/publications/internal-audit-assuring-data-security-privacy.jhtml, Accessed 9 October 2012.

Forrester and Seeburger. (2013). 'The future of data security and privacy: Controlling big data'. In: The WebCast, *The Silent Enemy: Preventing Data Breaches from Insiders*, 13 March 2013 at 13:00–14:00 EDT.

Hinds, J. (2007). *Tackling Staff Fraud and Dishonesty: Managing and Mitigating the Risks*. London: Chartered Institute of Personnel and Development Guide.

Hutchins, E.M., Cloppert, M.J. and Amin, R.M. (2010). 'Intelligence-driven computer network defence informed by analysis of adversary campaigns and intrusion kill chains'. Available: http://www.ciosummits.com/LM-White-Paper-Intel-Driven-Defense.pdf, Accessed 29 July 2013.

PriceWaterCoopers (PWC). (2014). 'Information Security Breach Survey (ISBS) technical report'. Available: https://www.gov.uk/government/uploads/system/uploads/attachment_data/file/307296/bis-14–767-information-security-breaches-survey-2014-technical-report-revision1.pdf, Accessed 2 April 2014.

Rosenberg, B. (2010). 'Defence Advanced Research Projects Agency (DARPA) build Cyber Range to test security measures'. GCN: Technology, Tools and Tactics for Public Sector IT Special Report, Available at: http://gcn.com/articles/2010/06/07/defense-it-1-cyber-range.aspx]; Accessed on 31 January 2013.

SANS Critical Security Controls. (2008). 'Critical security controls for effective cyber defence'. Available: http://www.sans.org/critical-security-controls/, Accessed 20 April 2013.

TechNet Blogs. (2013). 'Introducing Enhanced Mitigation Experience Toolkit (EMET) 4.1'. Available: http://blogs.technet.com/b/srd/archive/2013/11/12/introducing-enhanced-mitigation-experience-toolkit-emet-4–1.aspx, Accessed 22 December 2013.

UK Fraud Advisory Panel. (2011). 'Fraud Facts, Information for Individuals' (2nd edn). 1, pp. 1–2. Available at: https://www.fraudadvisorypanel.org/wp-content/uploads/2015/04/Fraud-Facts-1I-Identity-Fraud-Revised-Sep11.pdf, Issue 1 September 2011 (2nd edition).

Verizon. (2013). 'Data breach investigation report'. Available: http://www.verizonenterprise.com/resources/reports/dbir-series-why-businesses-are-attacked_en_xg.pdf, Accessed 27 December 2013.

Verizon, (2014). 'Data Breach Investigation Report'. Available: rp_Verizon-DBIR-2014_en_xg%20.pdf, Accessed 3 May 2014.

Verizon RISK Team Survey Report. (2012). 'Data breach investigations report'. Available: http://www.verizonbusiness.com/resources/reports/rp_data-breach-investigations-report2012_en_xg.pdf, Accessed 23 April 2013.

10 Summary of the Guide

10.1. FINAL THOUGHTS OF THE CHAPTERS

This book sets out nine essential reference guides and principles that can be used by crime prevention practitioners, security managers, criminologists, HR personnel and researchers for effective prevention of internal information theft in retail businesses.

Chapter 1 has provided an understanding of internal information theft in the context of retail business. Internal information theft has been identified, in most cases, as a deliberate stealing of business/customer information as a result of employees being overly trusted with few security and crime prevention controls.

Chapter 2 provided an analysis of the characteristics of perpetrators of internal information in retail businesses. It answered basic questions related to how and when internal information theft-related crimes are perpetrated, who perpetrates the crimes and why. Some of the answers to the question of when are: during retail business operations and during maintenance. As for the question of why information thefts are perpetrated, the common answers include for financial gains and through rationalisation. The methods of perpetration include use of legitimate system commands; exploitation of known or newly discovered design flaws in systems; collaboration; coercion; infiltration and social engineering. And the perpetrators can be managers, employees or technicians. In summary a perpetrator of internal information theft can be described as follows:

- trusted insider who abuses his trust to disrupt operations, corrupt data, exfiltrate sensitive information, or compromise an IT (information technology) system, causing loss or damage;
- can be a current or former employee, contractor, or other business partner who has or had authorized access to an organization's network, system, or data and intentionally exceeded or misused that access in a manner that negatively affected the confidentiality, integrity, or availability of the companies' information or information systems;

- an employee (manager, shop-floor employee or other "member") of a host company that operates a computer system to which the insider has legitimate access;
- an associate, contractor, business partner, supplier, computer maintenance technician, guest, or someone else who has a formal or informal business relationship with the company;
- anyone authorised to perform certain activities, for example, a company's customer who uses the company's system to access his or her account;
- anyone properly identified and authenticated to the system including, perhaps, someone masquerading as a legitimate insider, or someone to whom an insider has given access (for example by sharing a password)
- a former insider, now using previously conferred access credentials not revoked when the insider status ended or using access credentials secretly created while an insider to give access later;
- someone duped or coerced by an outsider to perform actions on the outsider's behalf.
- when a criminal uses a fraudulently obtained card or card details, along with stolen personal information, to open or take over a card account held in someone else's name.

COMMON FORMS OF INTERNAL INFORMATION THEFT DERIVED FROM THE CASE ANALYSIS

- Unauthorized extraction, duplication, or exfiltration of data;
- Unauthorised tampering (destruction and deletion of critical assets of data or records)
- Downloading from unauthorized sources or use of pirated software which might contain backdoors or malicious code;
- Eavesdropping and packet sniffing and spoofing and impersonating other users;
- Social engineering attacks via collaboration and collusion;
- Misuse of resources for non-business related or unauthorized activities;
- Purposefully installing malicious software

COMMON CHARACTERISTICS OF INTERNAL INFORMATION THEFT DERIVED FROM THE CASE ANALYSIS

- Actions were planned;
- Motivation was financial gain;
- Information theft acts were perpetrated while on the job;
- Information theft cases were usually detected by non-security personnel;
- Information cases were usually detected through manual procedures;
- Most internal information theft acts required little technical sophistication.

Table 10.1 Summary of the Nature of Internal Information Theft

Impact of information theft	Causes and motivations for internal information theft	Methods of information theft
Financial costs: huge budget allocation goes into job recruitment, training, data security, software security, investigation, court and information security auditing; • Losses: loss of customers trust; job loss; damage to business name. • Inestimable cost and loss: the actual records of approximate loss and cost may not be quantified.	• Financial gain: perpetrators use the stolen data for commercial or monetary gain e.g., opening a bank account, applying for a loan/credit card, to obtain goods or access facilities or services; • Cost of data security: human weaknesses in relation to conflicting operation demands they are being placed upon; • Socio-economic issues: family issues and cultural backgrounds; lifestyle, personal issues such as vicissitudes; • Vulnerability of data security: leakages, loss of gadgets, misplaced or forgotten access paths and complexity of security operation; • Availability of customer data because of business operations and processes using cards.	• Stealing with paper, pen, wallet, recording, typing and copying; • Redirecting customers order to different address, selling of the data on the black market; • organised crime—collusion, collaboration and infiltration, computer means, hacking; • Research of customers 'personal information', buying customer data from employees with unrestricted access

Chapter 3 explains the operations of retail business and the implications for internal information theft prevention. This chapter has provided knowledge of the roles management plays as people in the prevention of internal information theft and discussed how people, process and technology can be integrated to implement effective internal information security. A more technologically advanced retail company with better information processing guided by effective security management is more capable of preventing internal information theft than one without.

The integrated security and governance systems in smaller retail companies are generally weak. Indeed, the governance of some companies remains problematic, with lack of managements and inappropriate focus on critical security issues. There are requirements in some company data protection policies for employees to comply with but there is rarely substantial evidence that this is happening or that policies are being implemented effectively and monitored by security managements. Overall, they depend on technology-based software security neglecting the security capability of integrated security management oriented with people, process and technology.

Chapter 4 explored the available information theft prevention frameworks and their practical implementation issues. Most of the frameworks have attributed their failure to the lack of clear roles and responsibilities given to security managers and administrators. The generic frameworks and practices for prevention of internal information theft were not appropriate, although some (e.g., integrated security management and information security audit) have improved significantly over the recent years. The view of this chapter is that there is a need to design a comprehensive framework that would incorporate process, people and technology. And the independent use of software technology in preventing internal information theft is not enough. Nevertheless, the general view of this chapter is that checks and security controls in retail in relation to the prevention of information theft are still weak and need to be improved. The weaknesses in the system are at several levels:

i. The security practices governing mitigation of internal information theft—in particular 'at cost' requirement—are insufficiently robust.
ii. Mechanisms to identify and address the more intangible ways of carrying out internal information theft schemes (e.g., collaboration; coercion; infiltration and social engineering) in the wider system are almost non-existent.
iii. Some partner companies are not adhering to underlining security guidance/practices and/or are not doing enough to mitigate the security risks. This appears particularly likely in the younger, fast growing online retail companies.
iv. The capacity and skills of the outsourcing companies that work with auditing managements are insufficient to 'get below the surface' of what is going on (and in any case are not designed to be preventative).

Chapter 5 reflects on information security challenges in preventing internal information theft. This chapter explores the challenging issues of whether online retail companies have the capacity or skills required to fulfil their roles in preventing internal information theft. Some of the challenging issues identified are that neither the retail companies nor regulatory bodies (e.g., police, information/data protection regulators) are 'fit enough' with respect to guarding against information theft. The ability of retail companies to control intangible perpetration mechanisms (e.g., infiltration and social engineering) that do not involve 'much money' seems almost non-existent. Hopes that the law enforcement agencies (e.g., police) would address these issues are low. These are certainly that most challenging issues that will need to be addressed in relation to the new approach. The retail management should broaden their security capability and priority by aligning their roles with emerging challenges and implementing collaborative management. This effort, if implemented effectively, would counter the broader sense that retail company security system management lacks clarity of roles and is overly disjointed, from complementary managements to law enforcement agencies.

Chapter 6 explains the concept of collaborative internal information theft prevention and how this concept can be applied in retail businesses. Although the benefits and impact of integrated management overall remain contested, there is substantial evidence that collaborative security practices can work in addressing information theft prevention challenges.

The integration of people, process and technology has been proven to improve systems security where the independent use of technology-based software security has not proved effective. Retail companies need to intervene and adopt this new approach to secure their proprietary information. Security managers should take a bold step in adapting to the advancement of internal information theft schemes and develop a robust system over time: they should not invest solely on IT security, which might risk other projects, given the cost of advancing IT security.

Nevertheless, company policies demand that managers must be able to account for every area of business investment being balanced as intended. At present, it seems that interpretation of what this means in practice is largely left to the retail companies' boards and IT security managers to decide. Most worryingly, it seems that some essential prevention practices (e.g., security risk assessment, contingency plans and crimes investigation) are being signed off within the existing retail companies' policies to save the cost of continuing IT security maintenance. The recommendations of this chapter include key elements of a role-based model for preventing information theft:

- Management should be given clear roles regarding information theft, and these roles should be constantly reiterated;
- Management should be collaborative (e.g., sharing crimes incident analysis, risk evaluation reports, security audit details) in their functional roles;
- Integration of people, process and technology for any adoption of preventive strategy should be considered.
- Ensure proper education and awareness on the part of employees and customers towards prevention of internal information theft;
- Take issues of internal information theft as a corporate social responsibility to consult and engage with stakeholders and employees;
- Clearly document and consistently enforce policies and controls by instituting periodic security awareness training for all employees; and
- Develop an incident response plan to control the damage from internal information theft perpetrators, assist in the investigative process, and incorporate lessons learned to continually improve the plan.

Chapter 7 provided knowledge of the application of collaborative security management in selected UK retail companies. This chapter presents results of cross-case analysis in selected UK retail companies, to show the benefits of collaborative management in the use of an information security audit (ISA). It is important that management should review the current services which permit access to proprietary resources (e.g., servers, web application, customer detail) that are in their business operations and those that are contracted to partners and outsourcing agencies. This should include detailed analysis of whether existing security risks are indeed analysed and, if not, how the services and/or contract could be policed in practice.

Management should consider whether further steps are required to strengthen the regulations for data protection and security governance with partners. For example, we understand why outsourced retail companies often have to rely heavily on external security auditors, but we believe it should be possible for external and internal security auditors to work together. Ideally, no outsourced companies would take up the cost of auditors, but they should be encouraged to appoint part-time auditors to ensure sound security and share responsibilities with outsourcing bodies. The view of this chapter is that any such services and maintenances are potential security risks for employees and outsiders to collude, and should be monitored.

Collaborative information security audits involving cross-functional management can improve security and help to assess whether there are gaps in their roles alignments in analysing crime incidents.

Chapter 8 looks beyond practical implementation of security tools in prevention of internal information theft. It explores the application of crime prevention theories to internal information theft. The management should incorporate knowledge of other crime prevention frameworks across disciplines to tackle the complex and multifaceted nature of internal information theft. Because information theft is mostly motivated by socio-economic issues, the services of psychologists and criminologists, for instance, should be sought occasionally to contribute to employee well-being.

Chapter 9 advises on the recommended security practices garnered from renowned IS security consulting firms and research experts. Information security strategies are practices that ensure that employees do not steal and leak sensitive/critical retail business information. The strategies include software products that can help security professionals control what information employees can process during retail operation. The managements should implement the key technical security and monitoring processes, which include:

- Log, monitor, and audit employee online actions;
- Restrict access to personal identifiable data/information;
- Pay special attention to those in special positions of trust and authority with relatively easy ability to perpetrate high value crimes (e.g., desk staffers, accountants and managers).

10.2 RECOMMENDATIONS FOR SECURITY AND CRIME PREVENTION MANAGEMENT

The recommendations are meant to direct IT security and crime prevention managements to lessons drawn from information theft case analysis and strategic data security practices. Thus, the recommendations are focused on the specific issues on how to prevent and minimise occurrences of internal information theft. Thus, the recommendations focused on the more specific issue of how to prevent and minimise occurrences of internal information theft:

1. **Proactive information security and control:** Management should recognise the personal predispositions of their employees/contractors and understand the impact they have on internal security risks.

   First, retail companies should manage the expectation of employees to minimise unmet expectation. This can be achieved through communication between managers and employees in the form of regular employee reviews, taking action to address employee dissatisfaction when possible and consistent enforcement of policies for all employees so that individual employees do not come to feel that they are above the rules or that the rules are unjustly applied. When the expectations of the insiders are in line with the retail practices and policies, unmet expectations are not an issue.

   Second, companies can institute an acceptable use policy, describing the employee's roles and responsibilities when using the company's information systems. The policy should be given to each employee as part of their orientation. As changes to the policy occur, employees need to be made aware of the changes and the impact to them. In addition, the policy should be consistently enforced for all employees so that no employees may feel that they are above the rules.

   Third, managers, in conjunction with Human Resources, can clearly define job responsibilities for each employee. Processes such as performance reviews can be used to check and set expectations periodically.

   The management should review the current services which permit access to proprietary resources (e.g., servers, web application, customer detail) being contracted to partners and outsourcing agencies. This should include detailed analysis of whether existing security risks are indeed analysed and, if not, how the services and/or contract could be policed in practice. Our view is that any such services and maintenances are potential information theft risks for employees and outsiders to collude, and should be monitored;

2. *Handling employees' disgruntlement through effective intervention:* As retail companies discover the behavioural precursors exhibited by dishonest employees, they can employ positive intervention strategies to lower the disgruntlement of the insider. While the intent of employee

sanctioning may be to reduce undesirable behaviours, it may backfire in some cases. Disgruntlement increases, leading to more disruptive behaviour. When positive intervention is used, the disgruntlement might be reduced, eliminating additional behavioural precursors, as well as the escalation to technical precursor behaviours. The management should review the arrangement for the security and crime prevention team to assess whether there are gaps in their roles alignments in analysing crimes incidents. Our view is that poorly defined management roles can be a stressor for employees, and disgruntled employees emerge whenever roles go against their personal values;

3. *Targeted monitoring of employees activities:* It is usually not practical for a retail company to monitor every behavioural and technical action taken by each employee. However, a reasonable level of proactive logging of online activity across the organization's network provides data that can be monitored or audited for suspicious activity proactively, or targeted to monitor people who have suspicious activities.

Based on findings from the cases analyses, for example, periodic account audits could be effective in detecting backdoor accounts that could be used for malicious employees' activities. As the perceived risk of an insider attack increases, due to detection of behavioural or technical precursors, the amount of technical and behavioural monitoring should also increase. Enhanced monitoring could lead to discovery of precursor activity, enabling the company to identify individuals at a higher risk for criminal behaviour and implement more targeted individual monitoring. If a manager notices an employee progressing through the pattern of dishonest behaviour, he might consider an audit of that employee's online activity, and, if the actions are extreme enough, perhaps escalate the level of logging of that employee's online activity. Note that policies should be in place in advance of such targeted monitoring; an organization should not perform these actions without consulting with their legal department in advance.

4. **Removing forgotten/unknown access paths to information systems:** A company's full awareness of access paths available to an insider is critical to being able to disable those access paths when needed. Literature on the management of risks of information theft suggested two issues of data theft through access paths: access paths known to companies and access paths unknown to organisations. Management or the IT staff may forget about known paths, making them unknown. The forgetting path represents access paths which can be moved from the known to the unknown category. For example, an IT security manager might authorize a software developer's request for the system administrator password during a time of heavy development.

Therefore, the system administrator password is an access path known to the organization at that point in time. If a formal list of employees with access to that password is not maintained, the manager could forget that decision over time. The manager may also simply resign from the company, leaving no "organizational memory" of the decision to share the system administrator password. In either case, the system administrator password has now become an access path unknown to the company. Similarly, the IT staff may discover unknown paths, making them known. Access paths can be discovered by monitoring network traffic or by computer system account auditing, for example. Monitoring network traffic allows discovering suspicious network traffic for further investigation. Account auditing allows discovering unauthorized accounts directly;

5. **Effective measures should be implemented during employment termination/demotion:** Termination or demotion was the final precipitating event in many cases we examined. It is important that organizations recognize that such precipitating events may cause the insider to take technical actions to set up and carry out the attack possibly using previously acquired unknown access paths. A clearly defined process for demotions and terminations in combination with proactive IT best practices for detecting unknown access paths and eliminating unauthorized access paths can reduce the dishonest employee's ability and/ or desire to attack the organization. Prior to the demotion or termination, companies should be certain about what access paths are available to the employees. If the employee role is to be terminated, the company must disable all access paths prior to notifying the insider of the action. It is important to understand that if the company has been lax in tracking and managing access paths, it could be too late to confidently demote or terminate an employee without fear of retribution.

    When a demotion occurs, the company should analyse the roles and responsibilities of the new position and update authorization levels and access controls, including role-based access. Some organizations in the cases we analysed overlooked the change in privileges, allowing the employee to retain privileges from their previous position, giving them access to information beyond that needed for their new position. In addition, expectation setting during a demotion or termination can be a deterrent against future attacks. The employee should be clearly told what the acceptable use policy is regarding their new position, what their roles and responsibilities are in their new role, what their performance improvement plan is (if one exists), and that future monitoring and auditing will be implemented to measure job performance against individual and organizational goals and objectives;

6. **Effective Implementation of administrative checks and controls through HR:** Personnel (HR) rules and procedures for employees

include "soft" administrative controls intended to prevent confidential data leakage. Examples include a corporate customer privacy policy or employee ethics training. Background checks in theory could screen out employees predisposed toward or with a history of careless or dishonest behaviour. However, our case analyses and reports from the literature have shown that some convicted inside criminals had prior arrests, throwing the efficacy of background checks into doubt. Corporate security or privacy policies may attempt to prescribe correct handling of sensitive information. However policies that aren't supported by clear procedures, training, and tools are generally doomed to be ineffective or disregarded. The managements should consider whether further steps are required to strengthen the regulations for data protection and security governance with partners.

> For example, we understand why outsourced retail companies often have to rely heavily on external security auditors, but we believe it should be possible for external and internal security auditor to work together. Ideally, no outsourced companies would take up the cost of auditors, but they should be encouraged to appoint part-time auditors to ensure sound security and shares responsibilities with outsourcing bodies;

7. **Collaborative security and information theft prevention initiative:** The managements should conduct an enquiry session to understand whether the law enforcement agencies should be incorporated to contribute occasionally in their crime prevention forum. An alternative might be to require that law enforcement agencies become a non-departmental body rather than an independent body, thereby giving information theft prevention greater comprehensive consideration with managements. The management team should be multidisciplinary in structure to tackle complex and multifaceted nature of the crimes.

10.3. CONCLUSIONS

The socio-economic and security impacts of internal information theft overall remain high. However, there is a strong argument that security and crime prevention managements are working hard to address the impact on retail companies that face real challenges and where the IT security has not proved effective. It seems strategic that IT security and crime prevention management need cooperation of other management bodies to intervene and make decisions in the interest of customers and to secure online transactions. Equally, there is a universal recognition that information theft is not restricted to 'within' the retail environment: there are numerous examples of internal information theft cases that involved external parties (e.g., outsourcing agents, contractors and criminal gangs via collaboration, social engineering, coercion and collusion). Any consideration of ways to prevent internal information theft in retail companies should aim for an appropriate integration between software security and human-oriented security. This integration would allow the devolvement of every member of management, which does not inadvertently prevent managers from fulfilling their roles in preventing information theft or from being incentivised to do so.

Nevertheless, the PCI DSS and existing legislation/regulations state that retail companies must be able to ensure that payment card data is kept safe both during and after transactions.

At present, it seems that the interpretation of what this means in practice is largely left to individual retail companies and their managements to decide. The frameworks and systems for guiding and regulating how they do that are being challenged more than they were a few years ago; more so, the general sense from both the literature and evidence collected for this study is that the checks and balances are still weak. This is partly because the capacity and skills of IT security and crime prevention management are insufficient to deal with the sheer number of internal information incidents in retail companies.

In addition, the analyses of internal information theft cases suggest that many employees' dishonest acts are being signed off due to overdependence on software security and management oversight.

Meanwhile, the contribution of managements in preventing internal information theft remains challenging, with too vague roles and inappropriate focus on exclusively technical software security. Over time, researchers and security experts may be able to discern more integrated and structured management approaches for effective information theft prevention in retail businesses. For example need to ask the question of whether more distributed internal security decision making across member management reduces the risk of information theft or not. Hope is high that security and crime prevention managers will apply the analyses and recommendations of this book to address the multifaceted challenges of internal information theft, not only in retail business, but across other business sectors.

FURTHER READINGS

Anti-Phishing Working Group (APWG). (2014). 'Phishing activity trends report: Unifying the global response to cybercrime, 1st Quarter, 2014'. Available: http://docs.apwg.org/reports/apwg_trends_report_q1_2014.pdf, Accessed 10 June 2014.

Association of Certified Fraud Examiners (ACFE). (2014). 'Report to the nations on occupational fraud and abuse: Global fraud study'. Available: http://www.acfe.com/rttn/docs/2014-report-to-nations.pdf, Accessed 20 April 2014.

British Retail Consortium (BRC). (2013). 'Retail crime survey'. Available: http://www.brc.org.uk/ePublications/BRC_Retail_Crime_Survey_2013/, Accessed 10 April 2014.

Cappelli, D.M., Moore, A.P., Shimeall, T.J. and Trzeciak, R.J. (2006). 'Common sense guide to prevention and detection of insider threats: Version 2.1'. Report of Carnegie Mellon University, CyLab, and the Internet Security Alliance, July 2006 (update of the April 2005 Version 1.0). Available: http://www.cert.org/archive/pdf/CommonSenseInsiderThreatsV2.1–1–070118.pdf.

CIFAS: The UK's Fraud Prevention Service. (2013). 'The true cost of insider fraud, centre for counter fraud studies', pp. 1–11. Available: https://www.cifas.org.uk/secure/contentPORT/uploads/documents/External-CIFAS-The-True-Cost-of-Internal-Fraud.pdf, Accessed 4 January 2014.

Financial Fraud Action UK. (2014). 'Fraud the facts 2014: The definitive overview of payment industry fraud and measures to prevent it'. Available: http://www.financialfraudaction.org.uk/download.asp?file=2796.

Haley, C. (2013). 'A theory of cyber deterrence'. *Georgetown Journal of International Affairs*. Available: http://Journal.Georgetown.Edu/A-Theory-Of-Cyber-Deterrence-Christopher-Haley/, Accessed 23 April 2014.

Home Office. (2013). 'Cybercrime: A review of the evidence-Summary of key findings and implications'. Home Office Research Report 75, pp. 4–20.

IdentityForce Report. (2014). 'Identity theft protection with identity force'. Available: http://www.asecurelife.com/identity-force/, Accessed 12 July 2014.

Office for National Statistics (ONS). (2014). 'Report for crime in England and Wales'. Available: http://www.ons.gov.uk/ons/rel/crime-stats/crime-statistics/period-ending-march-2014/index.html, Accessed 22 August 2014.

PriceWaterCoopers (PWC). (2014). 'Information Security Breach Survey (ISBS) technical report'. Available: https://www.gov.uk/government/uploads/system/uploads/attachment_data/file/307296/bis-14–767-information-security-breaches-survey-2014-technical-report-revision1.pdf, Accessed 2 April 2014.

Verizon. (2014). 'Data breach investigation report'. Available: rp_Verizon-DBIR-2014_en_xg%20.pdf, Accessed 3 May 2014.

Index